KEEPING FAITH WHEN LIFE HURTS

100 DEVOTIONS *FOR* HARD DAYS

JONI EARECKSON TADA

ZONDERVAN®

ZONDERVAN

Keeping Faith When Life Hurts:100 Devotions for Hard Days

Published by Zondervan, 3950 Sparks Drive SE, Suite 101, Grand Rapids, Michigan 49546, USA. by Zondervan. Zondervan is a registered trademark of The Zondervan Corporation, L.L.C., a wholly owned subsidiary of HarperCollins Christian Publishing, Inc. Requests for information should be addressed to customercare@harpercollins.com.

Library of Congress Control Number: 2025948012

ISBN 978-1-400-35189-3 (HC)
ISBN 978-1-400-35190-9 (ebook)

Published in association with the literary agency of Wolgemuth and Wilson, Inc.

HarperCollins Publishers, Macken House, 39/40 Mayor Street Upper, Dublin 1, D01 C9W8, Ireland (https://www.harpercollins.com)

Art direction: Jamie DeBryun
Interior design: Lori Lynch

Printed in The United States of America

26 27 28 29 30 LBC 5 4 3 2 1

Before You Begin

I'll be honest and tell you my life hurts. It's been hard ever since I broke my neck in 1967 and became a quadriplegic. I had big questions for God, but over time, he gave me his Answer in my Savior, Jesus. Knowing Christ, however, did not mean that living with useless hands and legs became easy. Nearly six decades of paralysis, and almost as many struggling with chronic pain, make it hard for me to keep faith.

Take my bedtime routine. Getting out of my wheelchair and into bed is the simple part. While I lie immobile, Ken tightens the lymphatic sleeve to rid my arm of edema, and then positions me on my "good" side with five pillows. He coils my catheter, puts in my mouth guard, tightens the chinstrap, and snaps on my headgear. He then connects the nasal tube to my external ventilator and tucks in supports for my head. He turns on the machine and fine-tunes the oxygen. After adjusting the ceiling clock, Ken finally hikes up the guardrail and asks, "You okay? You got this?"

With so much stuff, and the noise of the oxygen compressor, I can hardly hear him. But it's routine, and I know he wants assurance that I'm okay and ready to face the long night, positioned exactly right. The mask covers my mouth, so I nod yes. He leans down to kiss me somewhere in between all the straps, and says, "You can always call me."

But I hardly ever do. My caregiving husband needs his sleep too. Often in the night, to push away the panic of not being able to move, I relax and let the ventilator breath for me. I "say" breath prayers in my mind, inviting Jesus to participate with me in my suffering . . . so that I might understand more of what he endured for me in his afflictions. It's what my union with Christ looks like. I sense his grace and, thankfully, fall asleep.

That said, I am bold enough to say that I empathize when people hurt. For years I have authored books that help readers like you grasp God's goodness in the midst of pain. For when one goes through a strenuous ordeal, it is easy to lose faith. It is human nature to doubt God when he sends demanding trials. It takes no effort to complain and thus diminish the work of the Holy Spirit in your life. To keep faith requires grace as well as great intention to hold fast to his Word, pray, and cry out, "Oh God, I'm slipping, please help me . . . give grace . . . make effective the prayers of your people for me!"

If you have ever prayed that way, then I'm delighted to place *Keeping Faith When Life Hurts* in your hands. I consider this slim volume to be a treasure trove of the most thoughtful, impactful, and Christ-honoring vignettes I've ever written on suffering (and how to live with it). It is a prime collection of one hundred readings that

I carefully selected from the 2006 edition of *Pearls of Great Price*. I offer these handpicked devotionals to you, each one filled with rich, deep insights that will help *you* keep faith when hardships seem overwhelming.

What does it mean to keep the faith? In 2 Timothy 4:7, the aging apostle Paul says, "I have fought the good fight, I have finished the race, I have kept the faith." To *keep faith* is to continue to rely on Jesus Christ until the end. It means to endure. Press on. Hold fast. And not complain (Philippians 2:14).

In your most distressing trials, I want you to hear Jesus say—as he said to a weak and faltering disciple, "I have prayed for you . . . that your faith may not fail" (Luke 22:32). Peter's faith was shaken to the core, but it was not extinguished. Even John Calvin spoke of faith as sometimes being "weak and flickering." But still genuine. Oh, friend, take heart; Jesus is praying for you, even now.

So, may this precious book help you find the strength to cling to the Lord Jesus through your trials. You may hurt—and hurt bad—but the tribulations are not an inconvenient detour in your otherwise pleasant life. They are the main highway. Always the glorious highway that leads you to a sweeter, more satisfying devotion to the Lord Jesus.

Joni Eareckson Tada

Joni and Friends International Disability Center

Agoura, California

DAY 1

What's Up Ahead

Commit your way to the LORD; trust in him and he will do this: He will make your righteous reward shine like the dawn, your vindication like the noonday sun.

—PSALM 37:5–6

I sit so tall in my wheelchair that I need a van with a raised roof. The trouble is, I can't see the road. My friend Careen and I once drove from Chicago to Urbana, and I didn't see a single cornfield or farmhouse for three and a half hours! She kept describing lovely country landscapes, but it only frustrated me. I wanted to see. I'm the sort of person who likes to know what lies ahead. If I can't see the whole road, then at least a few feet?!

We are like that spiritually. We say to God, "If you don't mind, please show me where I am going. I don't need to see the whole road, but at least a little bit." We think our faith has to be supported by a bit of evidence. A hint, a signpost, a whisper . . . something to give us a clue as to what God is doing. We wrongly assume that faith is the ability to take a couple of puzzle pieces and be able to envision the entire picture. Not so. Faith that must be supported by the five senses is not genuine. Jesus said to doubting Thomas, "You have believed me because you have seen me, but blessed are those who have not seen and yet believe" (John 20:29).

Our insistence upon discerning what's up ahead is natural, but it is a hindrance to real faith. It's why God constantly encourages us to trust him in the dark (Isaiah 50:10). True faith means resting in who God is. He has charged himself with full responsibility for your eternal happiness, and he stands ready to take over the management of your life. He is wise and good. Trust him with what's ahead.

No ifs, ands, or buts, dear God. I trust you with the road ahead!

DAY 2

Heart Exam

If you have run with footmen and they have tired you out, then how can you compete with horses? If you fall down in a land of peace, how will you do in the thicket of the Jordan?

—Jeremiah 12:5 NASB

Would you like to know what you really believe about God? I'm not talking about what you say you believe, or what you ought to believe, but what you truly do believe. Would you like to see the truth about you that God sees?

Well, you can. You can actually know what's way down deep in your heart. And here is how: The next time you suffer, watch how you react. Watch what happens in your head and heart. Take an attitude check. Because nothing reveals the stuff of which your Christian beliefs are made more than tough times. Maybe that's why the Bible says, "Rejoice in suffering" and "Welcome trials as friends." Maybe it's because only then can we know what we're really made of.

It's what happened to the Israelites when they were in the desert. It says in Deuteronomy 8 that God caused the tough times to test them . . . to see what was in their hearts. Well, the fact is, God already knows what's in your heart. He just wants *you* to know what's in your heart. You may be facing some keen disappointments today: loneliness, a bad medical report, financial worries, chronic pain, or an important relationship on the rocks. It's hard. But it's also strangely helpful. Because when you find out who you are and what you really believe, you're facing the truth. And remember, the truth always sets you free.

What have your recent trials or setbacks revealed to you about your faith and trust in the Father? That insight wasn't meant to crush or discourage you. It's an encouragement to set aside distractions and seek him with fresh urgency.

Dear Lord, I'm so far from where I want to be in my walk of faith. Draw me closer to your heart this day, and help me to release my anxieties and fears into your loving hands.

DAY 3

God Means It

You intended to harm me, but God intended it for good to accomplish what is now being done, the saving of many lives.

—Genesis 50:20

I draw a lot of inspiration from the story of Joseph. Although he was never paralyzed, a lot of things happened to him that could be construed as accidents. There were plenty of unfortunate mishaps in Joseph's life, like being tossed by his envious brothers into a pit and left to die. But later on—after more mishaps—Joseph told his brothers, "You intended to harm me, but God intended it for good so that others might be saved."

I like that word *intended*. He is a God of intention—he has a purpose, a target, a goal, and a plan. God was a giant step ahead of Joseph's brothers, aborting their evil intentions to suit his own purposes. Joseph's problems did not catch God off guard, presenting him with situations he wished would never have happened. From the beginning, God calculated for Joseph to experience all these things. Why? For the salvation of others.

God is not a sweep-up boy who follows you with a dustpan and brush, second-guessing how everything will fit into a divine pattern for good. He does not put on a hazmat suit so that an evil situation doesn't contaminate his holy reputation.

Think of disappointing or bad things that have happened to you. God's hands stay on the wheel of your life from start to finish so that everything follows his intention for your life. This means your trials have more meaning—much more—than you realize. Your problems have more purpose than you can imagine. Not because God merely used bad things, but because God intended them so that others might be brought to Jesus through your example.

Lord God, I praise you that your intentions in my life are always good. Every "accident" happens so that somehow, some way, others might be introduced to the Savior through me.

DAY 4

A Borrowed Smile

For You have been my help, and in the
shadow of Your wings I sing for joy.
—Psalm 63:7 NASB

In a crowded ladies restroom during a break at a Christian conference, a well-dressed woman putting on lipstick turned to me and said, "Oh Joni, you always look so together, so happy in your wheelchair. I wish I had your joy! How do you do it?" Several around her nodded.

"I don't do it," I said. "In fact, may I tell you honestly how I woke up this morning?" Several women leaned against the counter to listen. "This is an average day. After Ken leaves for work at six, I'm alone until I hear the front door open at seven. It's a friend coming to get me up. While she makes coffee, I usually pray, 'Lord, my friend is about to give me a bath, get me dressed, sit me up in my chair, brush my hair and teeth, and send me out the door. I don't have the strength to face this routine one more time. I have no resources. I don't have a smile for the day, but you do. May I borrow yours? I urgently need you, God.'

"So when my friend walks into the bedroom, I turn my head on my pillow and give her a smile sent straight from heaven. It's not mine, it's God's. Whatever joy you see today"—I gestured at my paralyzed legs—"Was hard won this morning."

I have learned, as I hope those women learn, that the weaker we are, the harder we must lean on God. And the harder we lean on him, the stronger we discover him to be.

Where do you feel weak today? When you borrow from God the strength, courage, and joy you don't have, people can't help but notice. Just make sure they know where it came from!

Lord, be my strength today—not only in the areas where I know I am weak but also in the areas where I think I am strong. And may all the credit, all the glory be yours.

DAY 5

God's Longings

Yet the LORD longs to be gracious to you; therefore
he will rise up to show you compassion.
— ISAIAH 30:18

I have longed for many things over the years. When I was a child, I longed for my daddy's approval and praise. In high school I longed for a date on Friday night, good grades, and graduation day with a college acceptance letter. After my accident, I longed to be on my feet. My longings nowadays are often pretty mundane, such as hankering for a slice of something sweet and chocolaty after dinner.

The verse at the top tells us what God longs for: "The LORD longs to be gracious to you." The word *longing* is only used this way twice in Scripture—the other time is when Jesus longed to gather the people of Jerusalem under his wings. Notice something about God's longings? They are focused not on things but on people. His yearnings are never directed inward or self-focused; they are outward. Never does he express a longing to benefit himself. His heart's desire is to benefit his people that they might glorify him.

Oh, how different my yearnings are from God's! Too often my desires are about what I want rather than what I desire to see happen in others. How often do I actually yearn for God to be glorified and his kingdom advanced?

The journey of the Christian is to strive to be more and more like God. Take a giant step in that direction today by asking the Lord to cleanse and refine your longings. A good place to begin is with James 4:8 (KJV) where it says, "Draw nigh to God, and he will draw nigh to you. Cleanse your hands, ye sinners; and purify your hearts, ye double minded."

Purify my heart, O God, and place within me a passionate longing to know you better and to look out for the interests of others before my own. I long for you to be glorified in my life. I desire for your gospel to go forth into the world. I long for your soon return!

DAY 6

Choices

Choose for yourselves this day whom you will serve. . . . But as for me and my household, we will serve the Lord.

—Joshua 24:15

Years ago, after living with quadriplegia for a short time, I finally got tired of being fed at our dinner table. But as I tried to feed myself with paralyzed arms, I felt like giving up. I wanted my arms back! Wasn't there an easier way than having a bent spoon inserted into the pocket on my leather arm splint, then straining my weak shoulder muscles to scoop food on the spoon, and finally balancing and lifting it to my mouth? It was humiliating to have my food land more times on my lap than in my mouth.

I could have surrendered—it would have been easy and many wouldn't have blamed me. But I had to make a choice. Was I going to let disappointing failures overwhelm me? I decided the awkwardness of feeding myself outweighed the fleeting satisfaction of self-pity. It pushed me to pray, *O God, help me with this spoon!* Today I can easily feed myself. No, I didn't recover the use of my hands, but I was able to leave self-pity behind, as well as cultivate a little bit of humility. It meant making the hard choice many, many times.

My growth in Christ can probably be boiled down to one word: *Choose*. Choosing the right path is hard. Often we have to keep pushing through failures. Sometimes it seems easier just to ignore God's instructions. But Proverbs 8:10 says, "Choose my instruction instead of silver, knowledge rather than choice gold."

What a difference you can make for the kingdom if you will follow the lead of the Savior and "choose life, so that you and your children may live and that you may love the LORD your God, listen to his voice, and hold fast to him. For the LORD is your life" (Deuteronomy 30:19–20).

Father, every day is filled with so many choices. Touch my awareness, open my eyes, quicken my understanding to the eternal implications of seeking your heart and choosing your path.

My growth in Christ can probably be boiled down to one word: *Choose*.

DAY 7

Overwhelmed

No temptation has overtaken you except what is common to mankind. And God is faithful; he will not let you be tempted beyond what you can bear. But when you are tempted, he will also provide a way out so that you can endure it.

—1 CORINTHIANS 10:13

"Oh Joni, isn't it wonderful that God will never test us beyond what we can endure? That's a promise from God!"

I knew my friend Sue was looking for an affirmation, a confirmation that God would never "bend the bruised reed." As I nodded slowly, relief flooded her features. Sue had never faced the kind of mind-bending, soul-obliterating pain that now loomed on her horizon. But with the recent medical report and the prospect of a morphine-drip pump in her future, she was scared. *Surely the Lord won't give me more than I can bear,* she was thinking.

First Corinthians 10:13 is certainly a promise—but it isn't talking about trials. It's talking about temptation. The promise is that God will always, always give you the power to say no to sin. But when it comes to heartaches, physical problems, and disappointments—things out of your control, difficult circumstances suddenly thrust upon you—*you may very well be overwhelmed beyond what you can bear.* There is a kind of suffering that rips your world apart and leaves you bewildered and wounded. There are trials that overwhelm.

I drew a deep breath, showing my friend the context of the promise—and her brow furrowed. "But take heart," I told her. "It's when we are at the end of our strength . . . that's when we fall helplessly into the everlasting arms of God. That's when God floods our hearts with sustaining grace."

You and I may indeed find ourselves overwhelmed at times—at the end of our rope and beyond. But we will never fall farther than the palm of his hand. And where he has called us, his grace will sustain us.

Gracious Redeemer, I want to trust in you fully now, so that when the waves of trials come, I will trust in you then.

DAY 8

A Comforting Verse

And we know that in all things God works for the good of those who love him, who have been called according to his purpose. For those God foreknew he also predestined to be conformed to the image of his Son, that he might be the firstborn among many brothers and sisters.

—Romans 8:28–29

The idea of God being in control can sound alarming, but once we settle into the promise, it begins to feel immensely comfortable. But does his sovereign control even extend to evil? Wouldn't that put God and the devil in cahoots? Not at all. For consider: If God did not restrain evil, then all kinds of evil things would come barreling at us, uncontrolled. His decrees and ordinances shape good and evil in such a way as to warn us of hell, woo us toward heaven, and fit us for life here and in the hereafter—all inspired by his love, pure and passionate.

You can't ignore love like this. You can't sit on a fence or put it off until later. The love of Romans 8 begs a daily response. God is working all things together for your good today. Will you not participate with him through your obedience? Today you may be forced to make tough decisions, as well as choices in hardship. Today you may be tempted in a new area—a part of you that you thought was safe. God is working for your good. Will you not obey him and work for his glory?

When we say yes to following God, and when we say no to worrying or fears of the future, walls collapse, sashes are thrown open, and windows in your life are raised to let in the fresh air of change and transformation. One day heaven will arrive, and we will embrace each other, free of pain, and marvel how God worked it all, everything, lock, stock, and barrel, for our good. Until that day, until God drops the curtain on suffering, let's commit to work for his glory.

> Thank you, Father, for working everything in my life into a pattern for good. I want to participate with you and work today for your glory!

DAY 9

Believe the Lord

Abram believed the Lord, and he credited it to him as righteousness.

—Genesis 15:6

Sandy had just returned from Cuba where she served as leader on our Wheels for the World distribution of wheelchairs and Bibles. She shared some pretty amazing stories. I knew she wasn't exaggerating facts. She's not like that. When Sandy says something, I accept it as true. I believe her. Notice I did not say, "I believe in Sandy," but "I believe her." There's a significant but subtle difference between the two. When I say that I believed Sandy, I was basically saying, "I trust her; her word is good. I know her and have confidence in her character . . . I believe her!"

Abram in our verse today understood the same thing. To believe someone is to have complete confidence in the very fiber of their being—it means they are utterly reliable and truthful when they say something. Abram took the Lord at his word; he had complete confidence that God was as good as his word. Conversely, if Abram had merely believed in God, it wouldn't have meant nearly as much. Believing in God does nothing more than qualify you to be a demon, for even the demons believe that (James 2:19).

Many people believe in God. They believe in a Supreme Being out there—in fact, lots of pagans believe a God exists. Some even believe that the God of the Bible is real, but they still don't place their trust in him. In John chapter 1, Jesus is called "the Word." To believe Jesus is to trust in who he is. Do you believe in God for your needs today?

> Lord and Savior, I have every confidence in your character. You are utterly reliable and truthful. Today I am going to take you at your word even if doubts or fears arise. You have the words of life, and I am happy to say, I believe the Lord!

DAY 10

Be Engaged!

Therefore, my dear friends, as you have always obeyed—not only in my presence, but now much more in my absence—continue to work out your salvation with fear and trembling, for it is God who works in you to will and to act in order to fulfill his good purpose. Do everything without grumbling or arguing, so that you may become blameless and pure, "children of God without fault in a warped and crooked generation." Then you will shine among them like stars in the sky.

—PHILIPPIANS 2:12–15

If I were to follow the advice to "let go and let God," I'd be letting myself off the hook. A hands-off approach to my walk with Christ has never gotten me anywhere. God played the key role in my justification, and I have the responsibility to play the key role in my sanctification. These verses call me to be actively engaged in my own salvation as I "work it out with fear and trembling." Why the fear and trembling? If I become spiritually lazy—not praying or reading the Bible much, not witnessing or trusting God when I should—I am making light of the blood that Jesus shed for my redemption. I want to have a healthy fear of offending God and a righteous respect of what my salvation cost the Lord Jesus.

You have a responsibility to actively pursue the person God designed you to be. The perfect "you" is that glorious saint you will become in heaven, and you're called to step daily into that image. God has purchased you, and he is asking you today to be actively engaged in your own sanctification—you will have strength to accomplish this because it will be God who will be working in you to act according to his good purpose. Take a bold step toward your sanctification today and let God take care of the transformation of your character.

Lord, I commit to obey you today, knowing I'm stepping into the person you have saved me to be.

DAY 11

Bending Over Backward

For day after day they seek me out; they seem eager to know my ways, as if they were a nation that does what is right and has not forsaken the commands of its God. They ask me for just decisions and seem eager for God to come near them. 'Why have we fasted,' they say, and you have not seen it? Why have we humbled ourselves, and you have not noticed?' "Yet on the day of your fasting, you do as you please and exploit all your workers…" Is not this the kind of fasting I have chosen: to loose the chains of injustice and untie the cords of the yoke, to set the oppressed free and break every yoke? Is it not to share your food with the hungry and to provide the poor wanderer with shelter—when you see the naked, to clothe them, and not to turn away from your own flesh and blood?

— Isaiah 58:2–3, 6–7

God's heart intent is to alleviate suffering, and he is bending over backward to do it. He is moving heaven and earth to dry the tear, lighten the load, ease the burden, mend the marriage, give to the poor, care for the widow, stamp out crime, help the elderly, uphold justice, bandage the battered, and much more. God rallies us to his noble cause, but we often do not respond.

God longs to push back the pain through those who serve as his body, his hands and feet on earth. "He is the head of the body, the church" (Colossians 1:18). And "From him the whole body . . . builds itself up in love, as each part does its work" (Ephesians 4:16).

God has placed his work in your hands, and "we take our lead from Christ, who is the source of everything we do" (Ephesians 4:15 THE MESSAGE). God's directions to us couldn't be clearer. But we hem and haw. This is ironic since so many of us fault him for allowing suffering to be the world's status quo. (The quo wouldn't be so status if we got off our duffs and followed his lead.) Let's change that today!

Lord Christ, you are my head, and I take directions from you today. Show me how I can partner with you to alleviate suffering in my world.

DAY 12

Mangled Earrings

Therefore, if anyone is in Christ, the new creation has come: The old has gone, the new is here!

—2 CORINTHIANS 5:17

I once was wearing a favorite pair of gold earrings, which were large and square with a smooth, shiny surface. While I was on the telephone, one fell off. When I backed up my wheelchair, it wasn't on the floor. I wheeled into the hallway to look for someone to help me, and immediately I felt a clunk-clunk. The gold earring was impaled on my tire. My friend plucked it off, but it was a mangled mess.

I asked a jeweler, "Sir, could you please make the crumpled earring look like this nice one?" He rubbed his chin and replied, "Lady, forget it. But I *can* make this one"—he pointed to the smooth earring—"Look like your smashed one." It was an option I hadn't considered. After a few minutes of hammering, I had a unique designer original: a pair of crinkled gold earrings that reflected even more light than before!

When God allows hammering and hurting, he is purposing to transform us into something new and different. Like those earrings, we are the same yet poles apart. Best of all, we are better; we are closer to reflecting the light of Christ because of our weakness. The jeweler at the mall could turn a flawless earring into a mangled one, but only God can take a mangled life and change it into a life that reflects the flawless perfection of his Son, Jesus Christ. One day the hammering process will cease, and we will perfectly reflect the image of our Savior.

Someone has said, "God ruthlessly perfects whom he royally elects." In what way have your hopes or dreams been smashed? Agree with God to hold on to his wisdom and grace through the hammering. It'll be a change for the better.

Lord Jesus, I believe you are transforming me into someone far more beautiful, more complete than if I had never experienced pain. I trust you with the hammer!

DAY 13

The Truth About Suffering

For it has been granted to you on behalf of Christ not only to believe in him, but also to suffer for him.

—PHILIPPIANS 1:29

You will hear some believers say, "Although God can turn our trials into good, he doesn't wish hard times on us, let alone send them. What he really wants is to bless us and to keep us from suffering. The whole reason Jesus went through so much is so that we *wouldn't* have to experience hurt, pain, disappointment, or affliction." The Christians who hold this view are of sterling character—they study their Bibles, care about non-Christians, and show love for Christ in his kingdom everywhere they go. Nevertheless, the statement above is a hopeless mixture of truth and error, and it misses the core of why Jesus came.

First, despite Christ's compassionate death for our sins, God's plan—not plan B or C or D, but his plan—calls for all Christians to suffer, sometimes intensely. The verse above in Philippians is only one of many that points to the fact that we are to pick up our cross daily and follow in the footsteps of his suffering (1 Peter 2:21; 4:12). To encourage us, God will write light moments into the script of our lives, but without fail, some scenes are going to break your heart, some of your favorite characters will die, and the movie may end earlier than you wish.

God's plan is specific. He doesn't say, "Into each life a little rain must fall," then aim a hose in earth's general direction to see who gets the wettest. He doesn't wind up nature and then sit back to watch its sunny days and devastating hurricanes. God doesn't let Satan prowl about totally unrestricted. Do you feel as though God has taken a hands-off policy to certain hardships in your life? Right now, place them under his sovereign care. Commit to trust him with his plan for your life.

Lord of wisdom, Lord of my life, I believe and trust you with every trial in my life.

DAY 14

Suffering's Response

At this, Job got up and tore his robe and shaved his head. Then he fell to the ground in worship and said: "Naked I came from my mother's womb, and naked I will depart. The LORD gave and the LORD has taken away; may the name of the LORD be praised."

—JOB 1:20–21

God screens the trials that come to each of us—allowing only those that accomplish his plan, because he takes no joy in human agony (Lamentations 3:33). Such trials are not evenly distributed from person to person, and this can discourage us, for we are only able to see through a glass darkly. We are not privy to God's reasons. But we can take heart that every trial is ordained by God from eternity past, custom made for each believer's eternal good, even when it doesn't seem like it. Nothing happens by accident . . . not even tragedy . . . not even sins committed against us.

The core of God's plan is to rescue us from our sin. Our pain, poverty, and broken hearts are not his ultimate focus. He cares about them, but they are merely symptoms of the real problem. God cares most—not about making us comfortable—but about teaching us to hate our sins, grow up spiritually, and love him. To do this, he *gives us salvation's benefits only gradually*. In other words, he lets us continue to feel much of sin's sting while we are headed for heaven. This constantly reminds us of what we are being delivered from, exposing sin for the poison it is. Thus evil (suffering) is turned on its head to defeat evil (sin)—all to the praise of God's wisdom.

What is the proper response to God's wisdom in screening our trials and allowing particular ones—sometimes tragic ones—to touch our lives? "May the name of the Lord be praised," says Job in today's verse. Think of a specific heartache you are facing. Will you follow Job in his response?

Almighty God, may I not "waste" my sufferings today but see in my response to them any sin of resentment, complaint, or bitterness that needs to be confessed. I praise you for your wisdom.

DAY 15

A Hard Path to Joy

Fixing our eyes on Jesus, the pioneer and perfecter of faith. For the joy set before him he endured the cross, scorning its shame, and sat down at the right hand of the throne of God. Consider him who endured such opposition from sinners, so that you will not grow weary and lose heart.

—Hebrews 12:2–3

The path to joy is full of pitfalls, valleys, and steep climbs. That's the way it was for Jesus. But through all the hardships he kept focused on "the joy set before him." Jesus was able to endure his cross because he kept in mind the joy of reunion with his Father, the joy of triumph over sin, the joy of all his divine rights finally restored to him, and perhaps most wonderful of all, the joy of being eternally surrounded by the very people for whom he bled and died. *This* is why Jesus Christ was able to endure the cross and scorn its shame. All for joy!

It's very much the same for you and me. Our path to joy is full of pitfalls too. But Christ has gone before us, imparting to us his enabling power to suffer with him. Jesus assures us in Matthew 5:11–12 (ESV), "Blessed [or happy and joyful] are you when others revile you and persecute you. . . . Rejoice and be glad, for your reward is great in heaven." And exactly what is our reward at the end of all our hardships? Our reward will be to enjoy God with the same ecstatic joy that Jesus has in his Father. Oh, happy day!

Christians have no reason to be miserable or pessimistic. There is no room for gloom and doom when you're a believer. If your heart is troubled by pessimism or doubts, repeat the verses above from Hebrews several times, especially the part, "Consider him who endured . . . so that you will not grow weary and lose heart." This is the secret to finding joy. Consider him.

Lord of joy, I delight in your gladness today, and I want to honor you by taking up my cross and joyfully following you.

Christians have no reason to be miserable or pessimistic. There is no room for gloom and doom when you're a believer.

DAY 16

Godly Questions

Will the Lord reject forever? Will he never show his favor again? Has his unfailing love vanished forever? Has his promise failed for all time? Has God forgotten to be merciful? Has he in anger withheld his compassion?

—Psalm 77:7–9

One night when things got as dark as dark could be, when all hope seemed lost, I stared at the hospital ceiling from my bed and prayed, "God, if I can't die, please show me how to live." The prayer was short and to the point, but it left the door open for the Lord to respond. Little did I realize he would. For "the Lord is close to the brokenhearted and saves those who are crushed in spirit" (Psalm 34:18). Slowly, like a hibernating animal waking up, I felt something stir in my heart. It was a magnetic pull toward hope.

I began to sense an interest in the Bible. When I lay face down on the Stryker frame, I flipped the pages of a Bible with my mouth stick. I didn't know where to turn, but the Psalms intrigued me. When I read Psalm 77, I identified with those seven rapid-fire questions. The psalmist's despair turned godly when it turned Godward. The irony of questioning God is that it honors him. Honest questions turn our hearts away from despair toward the Lord.

If you (or someone you know) are struggling against hopelessness today, if everything seems dark, follow the psalmist's example. Gut-wrenching questions directed at the Lord are a way of encountering God, opening ourselves up to the one and only Someone who can actually do something about our plight. If today you are frustrated, use Psalm 77 as a path toward a passionate desire to comprehend the Lord. Something awesome has to happen when you choose the direct line to God.

Father, I do not understand why you do things the way you do, but I promise to bring my questions to you. Convict me if I start talking about you "behind your back"!

DAY 17

Praying the Word

As the rain and the snow come down from heaven, and do not return to it without watering the earth and making it bud and flourish, so that it yields seed for the sower and bread for the eater, so is my word that goes out from my mouth: It will not return to me empty, but will accomplish what I desire and achieve the purpose for which I sent it.

—Isaiah 55:10–11

On the previous page, I invited you to use the Psalms—especially the questions in Psalm 77—to express your emotions toward God. Something happens when we handpick a portion of God's Word to voice our heart-wrenching questions, "for the word of God is alive and active" (Hebrews 4:12). There's power in God's Word. When we search the Scriptures to find words to wrap around our wretchedness, we are speaking God's language. And God *answers*.

Jesus sets the example. When it comes to heartfelt questions and emotional pain, Jesus experienced both like no human ever has. He did not linger in the damp fog of Gethsemane. He moved in the direction of his Father and proceeded to the cross. There, he aimed his cries Godward, not choosing his own words to wrap around his wretchedness, but—you guessed it—the words of a psalm. "My God, my God, why have you forsaken me?" he groaned, quoting Psalm 22:1. Praise his name, you and I became God's answer to Jesus' plea!

This does not mean our questions get answers. It doesn't mean cancer gets cured, wars cease, and drunk drivers stay at home. But God will respond to his Word. Instead of answers, we will find the Answer. When we turn toward God in our heartache, he promises our anguished hearts will find Jesus. And he is the One who holds all the answers—and all the questions—in his hand.

> I turn to you today, dear God. I voice your Word. Thank you for listening. Thank you for moving in my life.

DAY 18

The Passion of the Christ

He is before all things, and in him all things hold together.
—Colossians 1:17

When I saw the movie *The Passion of the Christ,* I was struck by the brute cruelty with which the soldiers treated Jesus. Like a bunch of poorly paid drunken legionnaires, they couldn't wait to take out all their frustrations on who they thought was a stupid, luckless Jew. They beat and abused him mercilessly.

The face that Moses had begged to see—was forbidden to see—was slapped bloody (Exodus 33:19–20). The thorns that God had sent to curse the earth's rebellion now twisted around his brow. The back of Jesus' legs felt the whip—soon the body of the Savior would look like a plowed Judean field. By the time the spitting is through, more saliva is on Jesus than in him. When the soldiers raised the mallet to sink the spikes into Jesus' hands, it occurred to me that the Son of

God whom they were crucifying was the very One sustaining their lives! Someone must sustain their lives minute by minute, for no man has this power on his own. Who supplies breath to his lungs? Who gives energy to his cells? Who holds a man's molecules together? *Only by the Son* do "all things hold together" (Colossians 1:17). How amazing, how incomprehensible that the Son, the victim, is granting breath and being to his own executioners!

Close your eyes and think deeply on the things you just read. Consider so great a Savior who would submit himself to such torture . . . for your salvation. Think of the cost and sacrifice involved in Jesus' crucifixion. Then, commit afresh and anew to live on a higher, more sanctified level as you trust and obey him with new resolve. Praise your Savior for granting you breath and being, as well as life eternal.

> Dear Savior, I am awestruck that you did not turn away from the cross, but traveled the road to Calvary for me. May my life today reflect my love and devotion to you.

DAY 19

What the Son Endured

Anyone who is hung on a pole is under God's curse.
—Deuteronomy 21:23

The pain and humility Jesus physically suffered leading up to his death was a mere warm-up to the real dread he faced. As he hung on the cross, he began to feel a foreign sensation. Somewhere during those hours that his body was impaled, an earthly, foul odor must have wafted, not around his nose, but in his heart. He *felt* dirty. Human wickedness began to crawl upon his spotless being—the living excrement from our souls. The apple of the Father's eye began to turn brown with the rot of our sin.

From heaven, the Father roused himself like a lion disturbed, shook his mane, and must have roared against the shriveling remnant of a man hanging on a cross. Never has the Son seen the Father look at him so, never felt even the least of his hot breath. It was the wrath of God being poured out like hot oil on the wounded heart of the Son of Man. And the Father watched as his heart's treasure, the mirror-image of himself, sank drowning into raw, liquid sin. Jehovah's stored rage against humankind exploded in a single direction. The Trinity had planned it. The Son endured it. The Spirit enabled him. The Father rejected the Son whom he loved; the God-man from Nazareth perished.

This is who asks you to trust him when he calls you to suffer. This is the One who asks you to obey him when it's hard, when your flesh is itching to have a little worldly candy. This is the One who asks you to honor him when you face tough choices. Jesus Christ bore the wrath of hell so that you might enjoy a home in heaven with him, the Father, and the Holy Spirit. Celebrate this marvelous gift by trusting God in every hard thing, great and small.

Father, thank you for giving me the gift of your Son. May my life be to the praise of your glory!

DAY 20

We Always Carry . . .

We always carry around in our body the death of Jesus, so that the life of Jesus may also be revealed in our body. For we who are alive are always being given over to death for Jesus' sake, so that his life may be revealed in our mortal body. So then, death is at work in us, but life is at work in you.

—2 CORINTHIANS 4:10–12

Our verse at the top could sound a little morbid. We *always* carry around in our body Christ's death? We are *always* being given over to death for Jesus' sake?! A hearty and happy yes! Why happy? Because then—and only then—can the vibrant, joyful life of our Savior be revealed through us. And his life is revealed in us for God's glory, our eternal advantage, and others' benefit.

We carry around Jesus' death when we daily die *to* sin in the same way he died *for* sin. It means not taking a casual greeting like "How are you doing?" as an excuse to list every minor and major casualty of your day. Not using your prayer group time as an excuse to gossip. Not painting a picture of your marriage that colors your spouse as the culprit and you the hero. Not living like a martyr and making sure everybody else knows it. These are ordinary, yet important ways of putting your flesh to death with its itchiness to rebel.

Oh, to die to sin in the same selfless, patient manner as Jesus on his cross! Oh, if we could only see that refusing sin benefits others around us (just as Jesus was thinking of us on his cross). Then his life would be revealed in us—his profound peace, effervescent joy, and enduring hope.

Jesus, I need the power of your resurrection to help me "die to sin."

DAY 21

A Willing Captive

Jesus commanded Peter, "Put your sword away! Shall I not drink the cup the Father has given me?"

—John 18:11

I once read a heartwarming devotional in *Tabletalk* magazine about this verse. In John 18, Jesus declared that he would no longer pray that the cup of God's wrath might pass from him. Here we see our Good Shepherd embrace the cross. First he goes to the Kidron Valley—a place well known to Judas. Jesus would not be captured like a hunted animal, but, knowing Judas would intercept him there, he gave himself up in the garden without restraint. Also, Jesus openly declared his identity to the soldiers. Some may have assumed Jesus would hide behind his disciples and have to be forcefully exposed, but not our Savior! When Jesus stepped forward to accept Judas's kiss of betrayal, he powerfully and majestically declared, "I am." With these words, the soldiers fell back in awe and intimidation.

Jesus knew he would have to stand alone in the hour of his death, and he faced it with royal resolve. Even when Peter impetuously drew his sword, Jesus admonished him, saying, "No one can stop me from the task before me." Maybe the soldiers thought they would have to drag away a reluctant captive under the cloak of darkness, but instead they faced the King of kings who willingly took control of the situation.[1]

Jesus went to the cross with a complete devotion to obey his Father, as well as a heart full of love for his people. Do you have a difficult duty to which God has called you? Is the Lord asking you to "die" to a certain habit, wish, or circumstance? Are you following the Lord's lead reluctantly? Ask God to give you the attitude of Christ.

Lord Jesus, thank you that you laid down your life willingly for me. Thank you that you did not balk once you accepted the will of the Father. Help me to do the same today in every difficult situation.

DAY 22

The Kiss of Peace

And he arose, and came to his father. But when he was yet a great way off, his father saw him, and had compassion, and ran, and fell on his neck, and kissed him.

—LUKE 15:20 KJV

In the story of the prodigal son, the father runs to meet his wayward son and kisses him. What a poignant metaphor for the way our heavenly Father receives his repentant children! That sinners such as we should enjoy the kiss of God! What makes it especially touching is that Jesus felt God's slap so that we would experience God's caress. Think on this: The Son of Man endured the wrath of God so that we might have his righteousness; he endured violence that we might share in his victory; he faced rejection that we might be embraced in eternal fellowship with God. Psalm 85:9–10 says, "Surely his salvation is near those who fear him. . . . Love and faithfulness meet together; righteousness and peace kiss each other." And it's all because of Jesus.

"God promised to make the arrogant drink a foaming cup of his wrath, a reflection of God's furious hatred of sin. But the one who drank this bitter, foaming cup of wrath was Jesus. It is beyond our comprehension—the perfect Adam, adored and loved by the Father, was also despised by the Father . . . consequently, we are promised that we will never bear the staggering weight of his fury. It has already been poured out on the perfect human being—the glorious Son."[2]

We don't deserve the favor of God. *We* are the ones who should have drunk the bitter, foaming cup of God's hatred of sin. But Jesus took that cup before it ever reached our lips. We receive the kiss of heaven. Take a few moments to let this glorious fact sink in.

Father, Son, and Holy Spirit, I am amazed that you sacrificed so much for sinners such as me. My heart is humbled by your goodness and graciousness toward me and all those who put their trust in you.

DAY 23

Don't Watch the Wall

Then Peter got down out of the boat, walked on the water and came toward Jesus. But when he saw the wind, he was afraid and, beginning to sink, cried out, "Lord, save me!" Immediately Jesus reached out his hand and caught him. "You of little faith," he said, "why did you doubt?"

—MATTHEW 14:29–31

My friend Dan, a race car driver, was recently talking about a terrible accident in which a NASCAR legend was killed. The driver's car had been in first place. Slightly bumped, it appeared he overcorrected and then, in the next instant, crashed into the wall. I asked Dan if that kind of thing happens often on the racing circuit. "Oh yes," he said. "Guys in their cars get into a spin, get bumped, and they see that wall coming! I'll tell you, there's one thing they're trained to do. *They must not look at that wall*. Their training tells them to keep their eyes on the track, and steer out of the spin. If they look at the wall, they'll freeze. Your body just reacts—you can't help it. The answer is to concentrate every nerve on steering toward that open space."

That answer really spoke to me. Because lately I've been experiencing an unusual amount of aches and pains, and it's had me thinking about . . . the wall. *It's not going to get easier, Joni. Old age is coming faster than you realize, and boy, you'd better brace for an impact.* As a result of my fears, I've "frozen up" at times, worrying about the future and its problems rather than the present and its opportunities.

Paul writes, "Set your heart on things above," and the Gospels say, "Lift up your head, for your salvation draws nigh." It's advice worth following . . . or you just might hit the wall.

Lord Jesus, sometimes my life situation makes me afraid. I feel panic rising, my mind locks up, and my fears loom like a large wall. As best I can today, Lord, I will fix my eyes on you, and not on my problems and fears.

DAY 24

The Night He Was Betrayed

Strike the shepherd, and the sheep will be scattered.
—Zechariah 13:7

That night Jesus was betrayed, he broke the loaf and gave it to his disciples. When Judas stood to leave, the Master looked at him. Then, Judas slipped out the door. The dark presence that had awaited outside in the night now stole into Judas's very essence. For the next few hours, the most distilled evil in the universe would personally operate through the body of a disciple of the Lord.

Back in the upper room, Jesus spoke quietly to his friends; they sang a hymn, then it was time to go. Out in the darkness they slipped through a city gate, down the steep ravine, and up into the hill of olive trees—eleven lambs and a Shepherd in the night. Jesus left his friends to go pray against a solitary rock. Eleven men who would later change world history—some accustomed to working all night on their fishing boats—could not keep awake to comfort their Shepherd and Friend. There in the dirt in the olive grove, the Son of God groaned in prayer.

It may have looked as though Jesus was alone, but the bleachers of heaven were filled to capacity that moment, and hell strained its neck to see how this prayer would end. The Father gazed down and gave his sober nod. The Son stared back and bowed his acceptance. The torches arrived. The sheep fled. And the Shepherd stood to go to his slaughter (Isaiah 53:7). Consider this: Jesus was thinking of you that dreadful night. He remembered you as the whip lashed across his back. He thought of you when the mallet sank spikes in his hands and heels. Make today a time of remembrance, thanksgiving, and praise for your salvation.

Precious Savior and Master, I completely yield my life to you . . . after all, you completely gave your life for me, while I was full of sin and selfishness. May my walk today honor the sacrifice you gave.

DAY 25

Walking Through Walls

Though the doors were locked, Jesus came and stood among them and said, "Peace be with you!"

— John 20:26

Ever felt like you were up against a wall? Stuck. Stalled. Stymied. Smack-dab against a cold, hard, unyielding barrier with absolutely no way out? You can't go back, you can't go sideways, it's too high to climb, it's impossible to tunnel underneath, and there are no detours. What do you do? A friend once told me, "Joni, when you're up against a wall, the only thing you can do is start walking through it." Sound impossible? Of course it is! Whoever heard of anyone walking through a wall? Well, someone did. In the upper room, Jesus suddenly appeared in the midst of his frightened, discouraged disciples.

The door was closed, the walls were thick, and there was no entry or exit. But Jesus came in anyway. Jesus did the impossible. And he is constantly asking us to do the impossible. When we face the wall—whether it be pain, an emotionally unbearable circumstance, or a difficult situation beyond anything we've ever encountered before—God wants us to walk through that wall. As we take that first step into impossibility, we will find Jesus in the wall, in the most unlikely place in the most unbelievable circumstance. And in the interior of that cold, dark, unyielding place Jesus whispers, "Peace be with you."

No matter what my situation, I have the assurance that if Jesus walked through walls, I can too. Besides, I have to follow him. I have nowhere else to turn. And neither do you.

What is your wall today? What is the impossible situation that has been stopping you in your tracks and turning you back? Ask the Lord Jesus to meet you there—right in the middle of it. And then walk hand in hand with him through that wall to the other side.

Lord, if today you ask me to do the impossible, thank you for giving me your grace to do it.

Jesus did the impossible. And he is constantly asking us to do the impossible.

DAY 26

Bible Lessons

All Scripture is God-breathed and is useful for teaching, rebuking, correcting and training in righteousness, so that the servant of God may be thoroughly equipped for every good work.

—2 TIMOTHY 3:16–17

Discovering God's hand in your hardships is really a discovery of God's Word. Consider these power-packed verses that serve as a lens through which we can gain a clearer perspective on our afflictions. Psalm 68:19 says, "Praise be to the Lord, to God our Savior, who daily bears our burdens." This tells us suffering is used to increase our awareness of the sustaining power of God. Second Corinthians 4:7 says, "But we have this treasure in jars of clay to show that this all-surpassing power is from God and not from us." This reminds us that suffering allows the life of Christ to show up in our mortal flesh. Second Corinthians 12:9 says, "I will boast all the more gladly about my weaknesses, so that Christ's power may rest on me." This underscores how suffering completely bankrupts us, making us totally dependent on God.

Second Corinthians 12:7 states, "To keep me from becoming conceited . . . I was given a thorn in my flesh, a messenger from Satan, to torment me." This tells us that God uses suffering to teach us humility. Actually, all of Philippians 2:1–11 shows us how God uses our hardships to impart to us the mind of Christ. The Bible is jam-packed with lessons like these.

The only way we can gain a right perspective on our headaches and hardships is to spend time meditating on such verses. All Scripture is useful for teaching us heart-pumping truths like these in order that we might be thoroughly equipped, as we see here in Timothy. Meditate on these brief Bible lessons and rejoice today that God wants to conform you to his Word.

You are the great Teacher, Lord Jesus, and I thank you for instructing me from your Word today. Bring these truths to mind when I am confronted with suffering this week.

DAY 27

More Bible Lessons

How can a young person stay on the path of purity? By living according to your word. I seek you with all my heart; do not let me stray from your commands.

—Psalm 119:9–10

Oh, to live according to God's Word and to never stray from his commands! In the previous devotional, we allowed the Bible to speak directly to us regarding a godly perspective on our afflictions. What great lessons we learned from the Word of God. Let's continue! Romans 5:3–4 states, "We also glory in our sufferings, because we know that suffering produces perseverance; perseverance, character; and character, hope." We learn here that God is more concerned with our character than our comfort! Psalm 107:17 states, "Some became fools through their rebellious ways and suffered affliction because of their iniquities." This shows us that suffering can be a chastisement from God for sin or if we are rebellious against him. Psalm 119:67 says, "Before I was afflicted I went astray, but now I obey your word." This is a lesson on how obedience and self-control are learned from suffering.

When it comes to embracing God's will for our lives, it simply must start with lessons like these. Psalm 37:14–15 teaches us that suffering is a part of the struggle against evil. Second Thessalonians 1:6 teaches that suffering is part of the struggle in advancing the kingdom of God. Second Timothy 2:8–9 reminds us that suffering is simply part of the struggle as we give the gospel. Lastly, 2 Timothy 2:12 encourages us—endurance of suffering is given as a cause for reward.

Are you tired and weary? Do you feel overwhelmed by disappointment? God will strengthen your heart today as you ponder these Bible lessons. Ask the Holy Spirit to apply each one of these truths to your heart. Ask him to transform you by the power of his Word. And then, trust him.

> I hunger and thirst after your Word, dear Lord. Thank you that the Bible has so many lessons for me to learn.

DAY 28

Peace Be with You

On the evening of that first day of the week, when the disciples were together, with the doors locked for fear of the Jewish leaders, Jesus came and stood among them and said, "Peace be with you!" After he said this, he showed them his hands and side. The disciples were overjoyed when they saw the Lord.

—John 20:19–20

The disciples were huddled together, shaking in fear for their lives—doors were locked, curtains were drawn, and lights were dimmed. Suddenly, out of nowhere, Jesus appeared in the middle of the room and announced, "Peace be with you!" This was no happy-go-lucky greeting like, "Hey everybody, I'm here!" He wasn't offering the disciples mere peace of mind by his presence. When Jesus said, "Peace be with you," he pointed to the wounds in his hands and side for a reason.

For Jesus to gesture to his wounds was another way of saying, "Friends, look at these scars. They mean that the war is over. There is no longer any conflict between God and man. I have satisfied the Father's wrath against you, and the good news is, I am your peace treaty. These wounds in my hands and side are evidence of the price I paid for peace between you and my Father. Peace on earth and goodwill toward men has finally been secured through my cross. And the proof of it is, I'm here. I'm alive!"

What difference does the Prince of Peace make in your life? Jesus says in John 20:21, "Peace be with you! As the Father has sent me, I am sending you." The peace that Christ offers is not for our pleasure only; God is sending us to go tell the world that the war is over, the white flag is raised, the treaty has been signed, and eternal peace has been secured. The proof? Simply point people to the wounds of your Savior.

> May your peace rule in my heart today, Lord God. Give me courage to tell others they can have peace with God through Jesus Christ.

DAY 29

He Is Your Shield

The eternal God is your refuge, and underneath are the everlasting arms. He will drive out your enemies before you. . . . Blessed are you, Israel! Who is like you, a people saved by the LORD*? He is your shield and helper and your glorious sword.*

—DEUTERONOMY 33:27, 29

Jeff was miffed. He wrote, "Joni, to even say that God allows bad things to happen goes against his loving nature. God is good, and he has absolutely nothing to do with the tragedies and awful things that happen in this world!" I thought back to the early days of my paralysis when I believed the same way. But it made me feel less trustful of God, not more. God seemed to be held hostage by bad things—things that were happening in my life! *Surely the Bible has more to say about this.* That's when I stumbled upon Deuteronomy 33:27–29. There I found a sturdy, wonderfully awesome view of God.

He definitely has something to do with the awful things that happen in the world!

God is *constantly* protecting us from the full force of the fall and the evil and suffering that goes with it. He is relentlessly shielding us. Time and again, he drives the devil away and rescues us from his wicked schemes. This sin-stained planet would have ripped apart at the seams long ago were it not for the restraining hand of God.

Second Thessalonians 2:6–7 says, "And now you know what is holding [the evil one] back. . . . For the secret power of lawlessness is already at work; but the one who now holds it back will continue to do so till he is taken out of the way." The Spirit of the Living God is the One who is "holding back" Satan and the suffering he instigates. Moment by moment God is engaged with suffering, restraining it, and only allowing those harmful things to reach us that ultimately fit into his plan for your life!

> Lord God, bless you for shielding, protecting, and preserving me this day. I rest in your everlasting arms, for you are my refuge in this world of sin and woe.

DAY 30

Putting Pleasure on Hold

Lord, I wait for you; you will answer, Lord my God.

—Psalm 38:15

Have you ever had a cup of the coffee they serve in hotel hallways or lobbies? Early in the morning people at the front desk put a pot of coffee out on a little table with powdered creamers next to some Styrofoam cups. It's not the best-tasting stuff—and may have been sitting there for hours. Sometimes when I'm traveling, I'll spot the coffee, sniff the aroma, and often I'm tempted to scarf down a cup. If I'm in a hurry, I'm thinking less about quality and more about caffeine!

Ah, but if I know there's a gourmet coffee kiosk at the airport, serving up a fresh ground heavenly brew, then I say, "Hmmm, I think I can wait a half hour." I know it will pay off. I think of that which is higher quality. It takes a little self-control, and it means putting pleasure on hold, but I do it in anticipation of an even greater pleasure on the horizon.

This is at least some of what it means to "wait on the Lord." Waiting on God does not mean passive indifference—hanging around and doing nothing. It has more to do with saying no to impulsive, spur-of-the-moment actions or decisions, and by so doing, saying yes to something you know will satisfy much better on down the line. Those who have not yet learned how to wait on the Lord may tend to indulge in something immediate that only half satisfies. But Christians who have fostered a degree of self-control—Christians who know God better—don't mind putting pleasure on hold. They know something better is brewing down the line.

God is always worth waiting for. Take time to be still before him, seeking his mind and his desire for your today . . . and all your tomorrows.

> Lord, I praise you for what Peter called your "precious and magnificent promises." I wait on you today, believing what you have planned for me is so much better than what I could ever grab for myself.

DAY 31

First Response

Paul and Timothy, servants of Christ Jesus, To all God's holy people in Christ Jesus at Philippi, together with the overseers and deacons: Grace and peace to you from God our Father and the Lord Jesus Christ. I thank my God every time I remember you. In all my prayers for all of you, I always pray with joy because of your partnership in the gospel from the first day until now . . . Now I want you to know, brothers and sisters, that what has happened to me has actually served to advance the gospel. As a result, it has become clear throughout the whole palace guard and to everyone else that I am in chains for Christ.

—PHILIPPIANS 1:1–5, 12–13

This was Paul's first letter from prison to the church at Philippi. Obviously the Philippians were anxious to hear how Paul was doing. The apostle could have started off his letter, "I'm glad you're praying because I need it. The prison guards are mean, my chains are chafing, the grub is lousy, the nights are freezing, my bed is hard, I can't sleep, and the other inmates are bullies. This place ain't no picnic!" That's how some people might have responded, but not Paul. He was not about to drag the Philippians down with a long list of complaints. Rather, he strove to encourage the church with his prayers and to assure them the gospel was going forth.

Paul writes in Acts 20:24, ". . . I consider my life worth nothing to me; my only aim is to finish the race and complete the task the Lord Jesus has given me—the task of testifying to the good news of God's grace." His focus in good times and bad was the going forth of the gospel. What an example! Throughout your day, think of how your circumstances and encounters with others serve to advance the good news of Jesus.

Lord God, the good news is the goal of my day. Help me not to complain about my problems, but to see them as opportunities to share the gospel.

DAY 32

What God Wants

Set your minds on things above, not on earthly things.

—COLOSSIANS 3:2

This is what God wants—hearts burning with a passion for future things, on fire for kingdom realities that are out of this world. God wants his people aflame with his hope, a "consider it pure joy" outlook that affects the way we live on earth. God wants us to be "cities on a hill" and "lights on a lamp stand" so that everyone around us will be encouraged to look heavenward (Matthew 5:14–15).

A perspective like this doesn't happen without suffering. It is affliction that fuels the furnace of heaven-hearted hope. People whose lives are unscathed by affliction have a less energetic hope. Oh, they are glad to know they are going to heaven; for them, accepting Jesus was a buy-and-sell agreement—place your sins on the counter and get an asbestos-lined soul. Once that's taken care of, they feel they can get back to life as usual—dating and marrying, working and vacationing, spending and saving.

But suffering obliterates such preoccupation with earthly things. Suffering wakes us up from our spiritual slumber and turns our hearts toward the future, like a mother turning the face of her child, insisting, "Look this way!" Once heaven has our attention, earth's pleasures begin to pale in comparison.

What has suffering taken away from you? What has it diminished or robbed? Don't allow your heart to dwell on earthly disappointments. God permits suffering to draw our attention to heaven where that which was lost—and more—shall be restored. Suffering forces us to look forward to the day when God will close the curtain on *all* disease, death, sorrow, and pain. Until then, we have work to do! John 9:4 says, "As long as it is day, we must do the works of him who sent me. Night is coming, when no one can work."

Lord of heaven, turn my heart toward you this day. I set my mind right now on things above.

DAY 33

Rejoice Always!

Rejoice in the Lord always. I will say it again: Rejoice!

—PHILIPPIANS 4:4

Living the Christian life is so opposite, so against the grain of our human nature. When this verse tells me to rejoice always, my inclination is to be glum-faced, thank you. A little bit of whining, huffing and puffing, scowling and sighing is more to my liking. But common sense warns me it will only make things worse.

Philippians 4:4 is a triple whammy: We are to rejoice in the Lord *always*, and then *again*, rejoice with an *exclamation mark*. Perhaps Paul felt he should underscore the command because circumstances in Philippi were so bad as to make the exhortation utterly unreasonable. But Christians can be commanded to rejoice because their ground for doing so is not in circumstances but "in the Lord." The command may be contrary to our old nature, but remember it's not Paul's command. It is the command of Jesus Christ. When Paul insisted we rejoice always, he was no doubt thinking of the words of Jesus who said, "Take heart! I have overcome the world," and "Blessed are you when people hate you . . . Rejoice in that day and leap for joy, because great is your reward in heaven" (John 16:33; Luke 6:22–23). We rejoice not only because Jesus told us to, but because he himself rejoiced. And that's with an exclamation mark!

How can we rejoice in every circumstance? In chronic pain or cancer? In rejection and bankruptcy? The next verse provides motive, perspective, encouragement, and reason enough: "The Lord is near" (Philippians 4:5). You can keep a bright outlook in the midst of any hardship; you can have peace of mind and heart when you know that the Lord Jesus is close at hand. Think of a situation you've been grumbling about; choose today to rejoice in the Lord in the midst of it all.

Lord, I bring before you the circumstance of ________________. I purpose by your grace to rejoice always, and again I will say, "I rejoice!"

DAY 34

Shine Like Stars

Do everything without grumbling or arguing, so that you may become blameless and pure, "children of God without fault in a warped and crooked generation." Then you will shine among them like stars in the sky.

—PHILIPPIANS 2:14–15

The book of Philippians is filled with commands to be joyful in suffering. And to be joyful *always*. The verse above echoes this theme as the Spirit of Christ, through Paul, commands us to do everything without complaining or arguing. That means *everything*. Paul was writing to the congregation at Philippi who were facing enormous hardship, and the temptation to murmur or grumble must have been great. The apostle was not so much scolding Christians for their sour attitudes; rather, he had a bigger picture and purpose in mind . . .

Evangelism. Paul's heart—and the heart of Christ—was focused on wooing others into the kingdom. His passion was for the salvation of the crooked and depraved generation in Philippi. When we suffer, God wants his power to be displayed before those lost in darkness. By not grumbling, we become "blameless and pure" before others. No one can point a finger. This shakes a skeptic to the core. Nothing makes a scornful, cynical world sit up and take notice of God more than when it observes believers actually rejoicing in their hardships, without a hint of complaint.

"Do everything without complaining or arguing *so that you may … shine like stars in the universe.*" Paul's unswerving focus in Philippians is evangelism. Every admonishment, warning, counsel, and instruction is always for the purpose of somehow reaching others for Christ. Think of how complaints or grumblings may have diminished your witness to those around you. You will shine like a star in a dark world today as you put behind you any grumblings or murmurings.

> Lord Jesus, for the sake of your gospel, for the sake of the advancement of your kingdom, for the sake of this crooked generation in which I live, please convict me if I complain today.

Nothing makes a scornful, cynical world sit up and take notice of God more than when it observes believers actually rejoicing in their hardships, without a hint of complaint.

DAY 35

An Ever-Present Help

God is our refuge and strength, an ever-present help in trouble.
—Psalm 46:1

Nothing is more suffocating, more soul stifling than the feeling of hopelessness. When you've tried every option, it's despairing to think that you've come to the end of your rope with no aid in sight. Hopelessness breeds when we fail to sense God's hand in the hardship, or the presence of his help. It's demoralizing to feel as though God is off somewhere, distracted by the needs of more obedient saints.

Hope is built on fact. And the fact is God *never* becomes distracted from your life. He *never* takes time off from tending to your needs. When troubles come, he doesn't back away to allow Satan a free hand. The verse above assures that not only is the help of God available and accessible at all times, but *God himself* is the always-present help in every trial.

"God understands the darkness that we face. He is right there in it with us, 'an ever-present help in trouble.' The Lord of light is your friend in darkness. The Lord of life stands beside you in death. The Lord of hope is your companion in your despair. The Prince of Peace supports you when no peace can be found. The God of all comfort waits faithfully near you. The Source of all joy is close by when death has robbed you of joy."[3]

When we've hit rock bottom or are up against a wall, we are easy prey for the lies of the adversary. When we are emotionally distraught, we believe the lie that God has become a casual observer, standing at arm's length from our pain. Write out Psalm 46:1 and underline the adjective. God is *always* present with help and hope.

You are my refuge and my strength, dear Lord. When troubles assault, may I never be deceived into thinking that I am beyond your tender compassion. Thank you for being always and ever present in my trials. I praise you for being in control!

DAY 36

Heaven's Incentives

The one who plants and the one who waters have one purpose,
and they will each be rewarded according to their own labor.
—1 CORINTHIANS 3:8

The Gospels are packed with parables of kings honoring servants for their diligence, landlords showering bonuses on faithful workers, monarchs placing loyal subjects in charge of many cities, and owners of vineyards paying top wages to the lowliest of laborers. These parables teach us that God *wants* to reward us. God is the king and the landlord who has every intention of giving us more than we deserve. He takes great delight in showering bonuses and blessings upon us.

Heaven has its incentives, and as we remain faithful in the midst of pain or problems, we are not only accruing eternal reward, we are giving greater glory to God. God is worth it! The more faithful we are to him, the more our reward and joy in heaven. Our reward will be our capacity for joy, service, and worship. Whatever suffering you are going through this minute, your reaction to it affects the happiness of your eternal state. Heaven will be more heavenly to the degree that you have followed Christ on earth.

Gospel parables are reminders for us to remain faithful . . . to not give up . . . to hang in there . . . and to do so willingly and happily. God is more generous than we can possibly imagine, and he intends to recompense and more than repay every hurt and tear. If today you are lacking resolve to obey through tough times, remember—God is worth it.

Father God, I'm amazed that you want to reward us in heaven. Thank you that when you bestow heavenly benefits and blessings, I will have the honor and privilege of turning right around to shower the blessings on my precious Savior. I want to follow you here on earth ... so that I can cast more crowns at Jesus' feet.

DAY 37

Anger's Focus

He replied, "I saw Satan fall like lightning from heaven."

—LUKE 10:18

The first time I visited Birkenau, the Nazi death camp in Poland, I was asked to pray at a large memorial erected near the crumpled ruins of the gas chambers. People around me bowed their heads, but I had to first ask the Lord to show me what he wanted me to say. After all, millions of people were put to death just a few feet from where we stood. What could—what *should*—I say to God?

I stared at a piece of rusted barbwire at our feet and considered the evil that fueled those gas chambers. All I could think of was my disgust for Satan and his hordes. So I wrapped my prayer around Psalm 139:21–22, "Do I not hate those who hate you, LORD, and abhor those who are in rebellion against you? I have nothing but hatred for them; I count them my enemies."

There is an accurate focus for our anger over the injustice and violence in this world: Satan. He was the one who started the whole mess. He was the one who, because of pride, brought on himself—us included—every horror of the curse of Eden.

"Our struggle is never that we are too angry; but that we are never angry enough. Our anger is always pitifully small when it is focused against a person or object; it is meant to be turned against all evil and all sin—beginning first with our own failure of love."[4] Turn your anger into action. It's how organizations like Mothers Against Drunk Driving and Childhelp began, to name two. Today, find a way to push back Satan's darkness with deeds of mercy and love.

Father God, I resist the devil and his lies. I purpose to spread the good works of your kingdom, bringing justice and hope, help and relief to all those in need I meet today.

DAY 38

The Name of the Lord

The name of the Lord *is a fortified tower;*
the righteous run to it and are safe.

—Proverbs 18:10

Theological convocations are not usually scintillating. According to Dr. R. C. Sproul, they tend to be academic and sometimes tedious. But he will never forget one incredible speaker at a convocation at a prestigious seminary. The topic centered on Jesus Christ. The well-respected, elderly professor climbed the steps to the podium, cleared his throat, smiled, and then spent the entire forty-five minutes slowly repeating by heart every name and title of Jesus Christ.

Rock of Ages . . . Redeemer . . . King of kings . . . Bread of Heaven . . . Living Water . . . Son of God . . . our Sure Foundation . . . Good Shepherd . . . Fairest of Ten Thousand . . . Savior . . . Mediator . . . our Advocate . . . Alpha and Omega . . . the Stone the

Builders Rejected . . . Beginning and End . . . Wonderful Counselor . . . Friend of Sinners . . . Great Physician . . . Anointed One . . . Healer of Broken Hearts . . . Lamb of God . . . Prince of Peace . . . Blessed Hope . . . our Atonement . . . Mighty Fortress . . . Shelter . . . the Narrow Gate . . . Lord of Grace . . . God of All Comfort . . . Word of Life . . . Rose of Sharon . . . Lily of the Valley . . . Bright and Morning Star . . . Glorious Lord . . . Immanuel . . . Living Word . . . Chief Cornerstone . . . Creator . . . Ancient of Days . . . the Eternal One . . . Author and Finisher of our Faith . . . First and the Last . . . Son of Man . . . Almighty God . . . the Resurrection and the Life . . . the Way, the Truth, and the Life . . . Everlasting Father . . . Captain of the Lord's Army . . .

And that's just scratching the surface.

At the end of the forty-five-minute litany of the names and titles of Jesus, the entire audience was reduced to quiet tears. This is what happens when we focus on Jesus and all that he has accomplished. Today, meditate on each of these names—and more, if you have a concordance—and express your appreciation to God for all that the Lord Christ achieved on your behalf.

Jesus, you are my all in all. You are everything to me. Thank you that I can hold fast to any of your precious names or titles and in them find safety. For, indeed, the name of the Lord is a strong tower!

DAY 39

Flight Rules

Therefore, in order to keep me from becoming conceited, I was given a thorn in my flesh, a messenger of Satan, to torment me.

—2 Corinthians 12:7

I once talked to a pilot who described how he lands his plane in a deep fog. He has to be extremely alert as he guides his plane on what are called Instrument Flight Rules (IFR). He's flying blind, so the pilot must be totally dependent on his instruments and the signals from the control tower. He is extra careful to listen and respond to directions: check altimeter; check air speed; check flaps, yaw and pitch, navigation indicators, radar; check speed again. Suddenly the fog lifts, the pilot sees the runway beneath his plane, and the landing is smooth and safe.

The next day when the sky is clear, the pilot comes in for a landing on what is called Visual Flight Rules. Because he can easily spot the landing strip ahead, the pilot isn't glued to all the gauges. As a result, he comes in a bit too fast, which makes for a bumpy landing. The apparent ease of using Visual Flight Rules caused the pilot to be a little laxer, when he should have been just as alert.

God often sends a fog our way and we find ourselves "flying blind," unable to discern what's ahead. God does this so we will pay closer attention to the way we are flying through life. When I'm in a fog, when my thoughts are clouded and confused, I have to live my life on Instrument Flight Rules. I think—check mission, check attitude, check source of strength, check perspective on the day, check, check. If I don't live life using Scripture and prayer—God's Instrument Flight Rules—it'll be a hard landing at the end of a bumpy day.

Feeling under the fog? Make doubly sure you are dependent on prayer and God's Word to guide you through the day.

Father God, please keep me from becoming conceited. Keep me from being too sure of myself. Keep me utterly dependent on you.

DAY 40

Stay on Course

Whether you turn to the right or to the left, your ears will hear a voice behind you, saying, "This is the way; walk in it."

—Isaiah 30:21

Ken and I were standing with a group of friends on a high bluff, overlooking Chesapeake Bay, when we got into a friendly argument about directions. One person stabbed his finger in the air and said, "*That* is south." Another countered, "No, it isn't. I would swear that's due east." Others threw in their two cents' worth, and people began to take sides, becoming entrenched in their opinions.

Finally Ken reached into his duffle bag and said, "I'll solve this one fast." Within seconds the compass confirmed that we had been facing west the whole time. And you know what? Not one of us was about to argue with the compass. We knew it had the final say. In the same way, if we only look at circumstances around us, we can easily become disoriented. Just a couple of wrong cues and our bearings can get turned upside down, making north look like south, making evil look like good. We risk dangerous wrong conclusions when we try to ascertain God's purpose and plans in our life using only our circumstances for cues.

I have never forgotten that lesson. The longer I am in this wheelchair, the more I need help in keeping my bearings. More and more pain encroaching into my life can turn my feelings "this way and that." I need the Holy Spirit to remind me that there is "a way I should go." Despite the backaches and headaches, I need to hold fast to the blessed Word of God.

As you walk through this day, determine that you will make no decision without first consulting the Lord. Ask him to bring Scriptures to your mind that will help you find—and keep—your bearings.

> Father, how can I be so foolish as to think I can plan my own life itinerary apart from your strong counsel? Guide me, O thou great Jehovah.

DAY 41

Being One in Christ

Now you are the body of Christ, and
each one of you is a part of it.
—1 CORINTHIANS 12:27

Last Sunday during Communion, I watched the plate of little crackers being passed down my row. I took note of how the well-dressed people in the pew ever so carefully lifted their "pinkie" and aimed for a cracker piece so as to not touch the others. My friend sitting next to me reached in to get crackers for us both. At the appropriate time, she lifted my piece to my mouth, and afterward, the other piece to hers. The fact is I just can't take Communion by myself. I'm forced to depend on another Christian friend to handle my bread for me. The wine too.

I used to feel embarrassed that I couldn't so much as pick up a cracker, but that's changed. I've learned to look at my situation differently. Asking for help makes me feel connected. Interdependent. One with others. It's a happy symbol of how closely I must live my life with fellow believers. I can't live my life alone and isolated. In fact, I couldn't even survive. Here's the point: Communion celebrates this sort of unity in the body. It's something we have to learn and relearn every day of our lives as we humbly lean hard on others for help. You and I desperately need Jesus Christ. And you and I desperately need his people.

You may not have any physical disabilities. But it would be a sad mistake to imagine you can live isolated and independent from fellow believers. Since we are one body in Christ, the hand needs the eye, the ear needs the feet, and the brain needs the heart. You have deep needs, and you are deeply needed. Remember that next time you lift the Communion bread to your lips.

Lord, help me celebrate my need of others in the body of Christ rather than being ashamed. And give me grace to make my brothers and sisters feel welcome and at ease enough in my presence to ask for help from me.

DAY 42

Two Lenses

Though he brings grief, he will show compassion,
so great is his unfailing love. For he does not
willingly bring affliction or grief to anyone.
—Lamentations 3:32–33

The Lord took no pleasure in my broken neck. Like any father who has compassion on his children, it pained his heart to see me hurt. Yet at the same time, it pleased the Lord to permit my accident. My spinal cord injury was something he sovereignly designed in and for his good pleasure.

God's ways are so much higher than ours. Dr. John Piper infers that God has the capacity to look at the world through two lenses—a narrow lens *and* a wide-angle one.[5] When God looks at a painful event through a narrow lens, he sees the tragedy for what it is. He is deeply grieved. In Ezekiel 18:32 he says, "I take no pleasure in the death of anyone." God feels the sting in his chest when a child dies of cancer or a husband is killed in an accident. When God looks at that same event through his wide-angle lens, however, he sees the tragedy in relation to everything leading up to it, as well as flowing out from it. He sees a mosaic stretching into eternity. It is this mosaic with all its parts, both good and evil, that brings him delight.

In the span of a single verse, the Bible asserts "the Lord brings grief," yet "he does not willingly bring . . . grief." God tried this out on himself. He willed the death of his own Son, but he took no delight in it. God saw how Jesus' death would demonstrate his incomprehensible mercy, as well as bring his people to glory. God often wills what he despises because—and only because—he has a wide-angle view on the world.

Lord, too often I have only a narrow-lens view of my world. Give me your perspective, and may I rejoice in the beautiful mosaic I will one day understand.

DAY 43

God Weeping

Jesus wept.

—John 11:35

When God looks at our suffering through his narrow lens, his heart is moved. Jesus wept at the graveside of Lazarus. He often wept when he prayed, pouring out tears in the garden of Gethsemane. Reading through the Gospels, it is clear that emotion choked his throat and empathy filled his eyes as he looked out on suffering people, like a shepherd gathering bewildered, sick, and lost sheep. Our sufferings matter to the Almighty, and he has wept in empathy time and again.

But heaven will reveal something different. There shall be a grand and beautiful mosaic, revealing an eternal plan that was never for a moment threatened, never in jeopardy of collapsing, and never on the edge of defeat. People whose suffering seemed confounding on earth will see this marvelous mosaic.

God will personally flip right side up the tangled embroidery of that scarred life to reveal the delicate and beautiful pattern never observed on earth. Those who have been martyred or tortured—the Christians in the genocide of South Sudan, Armenia, and China—will stand and adore God for his plan in their suffering.

We will experience love like we never imagined. This is good news for people who have never been "the most important person" in anyone's life. But in heaven, "all shall have as much love as they desire . . . as much as they can bear. Such will be the sweet and perfect harmony among the heavenly saints, perfect love reigning in every heart toward every other, without limit or restriction or interruption."[6]

Best of all, Jesus Christ and his bride will no longer taste tears (unless they are tears of joy?!). The grand and glorious mosaic—the wide-angle way of looking at life—will be revealed and we shall finally *understand*. In the meantime, Psalm 56:8 promises, "Record my misery; list my tears on your scroll—are they not in your record?"

Lord Jesus, your tears are very precious to me. Thank you that you wept on my behalf when you interceded for me and all those you love.

DAY 44

The Sufferings of Jesus

In a loud voice they were saying: "Worthy is the Lamb, who was slain, to receive power and wealth and wisdom and strength and honor and glory and praise!"

—Revelation 5:12

In heaven, not only will our sufferings win us merit, the sufferings of Jesus will have an eternal perspective too. Our Lord will be honored as the slain Lamb. His sufferings will *never* be forgotten. Unlike us, he will always visibly bare his wounds to the universe, and for that, God the Father, Son, and Holy Spirit will enjoy praise as never before!

If any dark demon in the corner of the universe ever doubted the righteousness of God in stooping to rescue debased sinners, he'll be set straight. No evil spirit will dare accuse God of having defiled his purity in order to redeem wicked men. No one will question God's righteous reputation for having condescended to save sinners. God's righteousness will be beyond question! In fact, the sacrifice and suffering of Jesus was of such massive worth and supreme value that God's righteousness will shine even brighter. For it will be shown that God in his wisdom was able to rescue sinners, redeem suffering, crush the rebellion, restore all things, vindicate his holy name, and provide restitution . . . and come out all the more glorious for it! Heaven will show this. And we will praise him for it for all of eternity.

You have something eternally precious in common with Christ—suffering! No angel or archangel will ever fully grasp the sweet union that affliction has refined between you and your Savior. In heaven you won't praise the suffering, but you will praise the wisdom and the power of God in using it to drive you to the cross, as well as showcase his righteousness and mercy for all of eternity.

How unsearchable is your wisdom, O God! I praise you for your awesome plan of salvation and the way you use affliction to showcase your mercy and grace. I look forward to heaven where it will all be made plain!

You have something eternally precious in common with Christ—suffering! No angel or archangel will ever fully grasp the sweet union that affliction has refined between you and your Savior.

DAY 45

For the Sake of Christ

That is why, for Christ's sake, I delight in weaknesses, in insults, in hardships, in persecutions, in difficulties. For when I am weak, then I am strong.

—2 CORINTHIANS 12:10

It's one thing to muster a submissive attitude toward God when we bring troubles on ourselves, but it's a different matter when unexpected trials hit us broadside—trials not of our own making. Like when a drunk driver veers across the yellow line. Or a grim-faced doctor diagnoses cancer. Or reassessment slaps your property into a higher tax bracket. Or a clumsy linebacker breaks your high-school kid's leg in football practice. Or an old friend drags your name through the mud. You didn't bring any of these troubles on yourself; these are circumstances over which you have no control—and for that reason, they're the hardest with which to deal.

But look at the apostle Paul. He didn't bring that shipwreck on himself. He didn't instigate a death threat in Damascus. He didn't orchestrate mob scenes that left him smashed by stones. Paul may not have been responsible for his circumstances, but he *was* responsible for the way he reacted. He never groaned, "Oh, for Pete's sake, here we go again!" Instead, he said, "For Christ's sake, I delight in hardships." Another response? He said in 2 Timothy 2:10, "Therefore I endure everything for the sake of the elect." These were the first words out of Paul's mouth when he was pelted by stones, blindsided by brutal floggings, and thrown into dark dungeons. He endured hardships for Christ's sake, as well as the sake of the church.

When trials assault you, bite your tongue from saying, "Oh, for Pete's sake!" Instead, whisper a word or two of praise. No matter what the circumstances at home or at the office, praise is possible when we win the battle with words that bless our Lord.

Lord God, for the sake of your Son, Jesus, and for the sake of my friends and family watching me, I give you praise today in the midst of my hardships.

DAY 46

The Graft

I am the vine; you are the branches. If you remain in me and I in you, you will bear much fruit; apart from me you can do nothing.

—John 15:5

As a child, I remember early spring and grafting time in my uncle Don's apple orchard. My uncle would run his hand over the bark of the apple tree, finding just the right place to peel it away and make a slanting cut into the heart of the wood. He would then take a small branch and push the graft down into the damp wood of the tree. Later that spring, new life would emerge: blossoms to buds to fruit. I've heard that one tree can bear over one hundred different kinds of apples. But it does not come without a wounding in both tree and branch.

Years later I would understand John Bunyan's words: "Conversion is not the smooth, easy-going process some men seem to think. . . . It is wounding work, this breaking of the hearts, but without wounding there is no saving. Where there is grafting there is a cutting, the graft must be let in with a wound. . . . Heart must be set to heart . . . or there will be no sap from root to branch."[7]

Never would I have dreamed as I wandered through that orchard as a little girl, sensing the Spirit's promptings to draw nearer, that my journey to know God would be filled with such cutting and wounding. The diving accident in which I became paralyzed was yet in the future, but it would force my wound to his wound, my heart to his heart. Years later I would understand the lesson of the graft: The wounding is where divine sap flows and spiritual fruit blossoms.

In affliction and suffering, our hearts are pressed into his. And the life of God flows into us, wound to wound. In those times of brokenness, remember that in Christ, the result is life, life, and more life.

Help me, Lord, to remain, to abide in you this day, no matter what my circumstances.

DAY 47

The Lord Your Helper

Jesus left the synagogue and went to the home of Simon. Now Simon's mother-in-law was suffering from a high fever, and they asked Jesus to help her.

—Luke 4:38

Picture the scene. When Jesus entered the home of Simon Peter and learned his mother-in-law was sick, the people made a beautiful and simple request. They asked Jesus to help her. No fanfare, no digging deep into the matter, no extended discussions and wondering if it was the will of God or not. Jesus was under their roof, and they knew he had the power to help a sick woman. And he did.

Sometimes it's hard to know what or how to pray. Ken and I have felt that way lately. For several months, we have been praying nightly for a list of friends who have cancer. Some of the cases are pretty extensive, others look hopeful. Through it all, our friends are struggling through pain and disappointment. Often we don't know how to pray, but we can't go wrong following the lead of Luke 4:38, "Lord, help her." It's simple, to the point, direct, and sincere. Jesus is under the roof in the homes of our friends, and we don't have to dig deep into the matter or question God's will.

There's something else I like about that simple prayer, "Lord, help her." It sums up our bewilderment. It describes how we've come to the end of our understanding and that we have nowhere or no one else to whom we can turn. To pray "Lord, help her" is to have your focus on Jesus. Whether it's healing in the here and now or hope for the hereafter, there's one thing utterly true of the Lord: "He is your shield and helper and your glorious sword" (Deuteronomy 33:29).

Jesus, I pray that you will be a help today to my friends or family members who are dealing with illnesses. I may not be certain how each sickness will turn out, but I know for sure you will shower your help and hope today. So be it.

DAY 48

No Tear Wasted

There is a time for everything, and a season for every activity under the heavens . . . a time to weep and a time to laugh, a time to mourn and a time to dance.

—ECCLESIASTES 3:1, 4

An old devotional book movingly says, "How can God dry your tears in the next world if you have not wept in this one?" The image of God tenderly wiping away your tears describes a loving and utterly compassionate moment in heaven between you and your Savior. Your earthly sorrows have a profound purpose in eternity: They are setting the stage for God to engage himself wholly and completely in your eternal comfort. No wonder David prayed in Psalm 56:8 (KJV) for God to "put thou my tears into thy bottle: are they not in thy book?"

God will atone for every single one of your tears. First, the reason behind your suffering will be made plain as God reveals something so glorious in his purpose that it will completely suffice for all your hurt. Next, as God dries your tears, it will showcase the intimate, sweet affection of God toward you personally—much more so than if you never cried!

I'm not glorifying weeping, but I'm glorifying the God whose purpose will be exalted and whose tenderhearted compassion will be *glorified* through your weeping. Søren Kierkegaard said, "In the language of eternity, the suffering that helped you to the highest, is certainly not useless. It is useless and unused only if you do not allow yourself to be helped by it to the highest."[8]

When time comes for weeping, comfort yourself with these assurances from God's Word. No tear will be wasted. Share today's thoughts with a friend who is grieving or hurting. And don't forget . . . bring Kleenex.

> Lord, I am amazed that you have recorded in detail every time I've cried. Help me not to hide my tears. Help me also not to waste my sorrows, remembering they are aiding me for all of eternity.

DAY 49

A Word from Joni's Sister

In him we were also chosen, having been predestined according to the plan of him who works out everything in conformity with the purpose of his will.

—Ephesians 1:11

My name is Kathy Eareckson, and Joni is my little sister. I'm the one who was at the beach that day when Joni dove off the raft and broke her neck. I will never forget that Saturday afternoon in July 1967. I was a teenager, like Joni, and had planned a swimming date with my boyfriend. I knew Joni had hoped to play tennis with her friend that afternoon, but when the match fell through, I asked if she wanted to join us.

We drove to the beach on Chesapeake Bay and wasted no time in heading for the cool water. I stayed near shore, but Joni made a beeline for a raft anchored further out in the water. Suddenly, I felt a sharp pinch. A crab pinched my toe! Startled, I shouted to Joni, "Watch out for crabs!" She didn't respond. In fact, she was nowhere in sight. Not on the raft. Not in the water. Something told me to go find her—*quickly*. I reached her just when she was beginning to drown! What are the chances of a crab pinching someone's toe and getting her attention just in time to respond to an emergency? A million to one. Every time I've been tempted to doubt God's hand in those terrible circumstances that day, God brings that humble little crab to mind. From the big events in life down to the tiniest of details, he is great, he is sovereign, and he is in control.

I've learned from Joni (actually, the Bible) that though our circumstances are puzzling, perplexing, and even heartbreaking, we can trust him. Bow low before the throne of your Father who loves you and cares about every detail of your life.

Praise you, Father. It's so amazing that a God who spins great galaxies across the void of space would care about the seemingly small events of my day.

DAY 50

Women of Influence

Neither do people light a lamp and put it under a bowl. Instead they put it on its stand, and it gives light to everyone in the house.

—MATTHEW 5:15

More than two hundred years ago, two average, rather frail women became concerned by the spiritual state of their small church in a little Minnesota town. They decided to meet together regularly and pray for God to work. A short time later their pastor noticed that his heart seemed more open to the Word of God—and that his preaching had fresh power. Several families in the congregation fell under conviction and confessed their sin. Other families began witnessing to their neighbors. Before long, people were traveling from far away to become involved in the many Bible studies springing up in the church community. Soon wholesale spiritual revival broke out, and God's Spirit moved powerfully across the state of Minnesota, changing the landscape for decades to come.

These two women never wrote a book or traveled to other cities to tell their story. They didn't even want their names known! But they were powerful women of influence, substantial saints who let God exercise spiritual clout through them. And you are no different. God is not looking for famous individuals who can speak eloquently before thousands. God is looking for someone like you. Daniel 11:32 (NASB) says: "The people who know their God will display strength and take action."

The passage doesn't say you have to join the talk-show circuit or do noteworthy things. If you know God, display his strength and take action! It may be as simple as taking a meal to family with a sick mom, leading a Bible study, or just meeting with a few friends to pray. First make sure you know him, know his heart. And then just do what he says!

Father God, I do know you and love you. Empower me by your Holy Spirit and show me how to take action—wherever and however you lead—to advance your kingdom.

DAY 51

Praise Him with Every Part

Praise the Lord*, my soul; all my inmost being, praise his holy name. Praise the* Lord*, my soul, and forget not all his benefits—who forgives all your sins and heals all your diseases, who redeems your life from the pit and crowns you with love and compassion, who satisfies your desires with good things so that your youth is renewed like the eagle's.*

—Psalm 103:1–5

After years of quadriplegia, my bones are feeling tired. But whenever I struggle with pain, I pray, "Bless the Lord, O my soul, and all that is within me, bless his holy name." I force *all* parts of me to bless the Lord, even my lower back when it's aching. It's one way of making certain God receives glory during physically agonizing times.

Physical pain can cloud our convictions about God's benefits, which is why I must continually stir my soul to remember them. God has pardoned all my sin, rescued, restored, crowned me with his love, and healed all my diseases. Does this mean the pain goes away? Not immediately, but I have the sure promise that just as Jesus rose from the grave with a new body, so I will one day rise with no more pain or heartache. For now, as Paul says in Romans 8, we groan, waiting for the redemption God has promised.

Nevertheless, our groans can glorify God! Next time your muscles ache, your head throbs, or your feet cramp, force these body parts to join your soul in praising God: "Praise the Lord, O my soul; and even my sore back blesses you. Every part of me blesses your holy name!" You will be stirring your soul to recall God's benefits. You will be offering a "sacrifice of praise" (Hebrews 13:15).

Lord Jesus, I want to praise you in body, soul, and spirit. I bless you from that part of me that "hurts" today. May it be a sacrifice of praise, for every part of me delights in every part of you!

DAY 52

We Were Made for This

I will say to the north, "Give them up!" and to the south, "Do not hold them back." Bring my sons from afar and my daughters from the ends of the earth—everyone who is called by my name, whom I created for my glory, whom I formed and made.

—Isaiah 43:6–7

Ever wonder exactly why God created you? Or why he placed children in your specific family? God couldn't have spelled it out any plainer than in Isaiah 43:6–7. God created you and me for one purpose: to showcase his glory, to enjoy it, display it, and demonstrate it every day to all those we encounter.

What does it mean to put his glory on display? It means highlighting his attributes and characteristics. It means making hard choices to do the right—that is, the righteous—thing. It means biting your tongue from gossiping, going out of your way for a neighbor in need, telling the truth even when it's hard, not snapping back when someone hurts you, or speaking freely and openly about your Father in heaven. In short, it's living like Jesus lived when he walked on earth.

God is invisible. In the Old Testament, whenever he wanted to display his character, his innermost being, he did so through something visible like a burning bush, a pillar of cloud or of fire, or a "theophany" (an appearance of the preincarnate Christ). In the New Testament, God displayed his glory through his Son, Jesus. But Jesus doesn't physically walk on earth anymore, and bushes that burn are only in prairie fires or piles of raked leaves. So how does an invisible God display his glory in this age? Through you. What a privilege.

Father God, what an honor I've been given! You no longer choose burning bushes through which to speak, you choose people like me. Point out ways I can showcase your character and glorious qualities to others today. In so doing, I'll be glorifying you . . . I'll be living the life I was created to live.

God created you and me for one purpose: to showcase his glory, to enjoy it, display it, and demonstrate it every day to all those we encounter.

DAY 53

It Came to Pass

But it came to pass within a while after . . .
—JUDGES 15:1 KJV

I was talking with an African sister in Christ in a small Ghanaian village. I was impressed with her quiet, humble spirit. She wore brightly colored tribal clothes with a turbanlike headdress. Although I guessed she was young, her hands were weathered and lined. After she shared her testimony, I asked what her favorite Bible verse was. A knowing smile spread across her face and her eyes lit up. Without hesitation, she replied, "And it came to pass." I gave her a puzzled look. She added, "Everywhere you look in the Bible, there it is, my favorite verse." It was a familiar phrase from God's Word, but I had never heard anyone claim it as their favorite. I asked her to explain.

"Joni, it is a hard life we live in our country. The weather is harsh and our crops sometimes fail. It's at those times we don't know where the next meal is coming from. We have no money, nothing to offer our children. But we have God!" she said in a hearty voice. "And we know he will take care of us. We can look at the misery around us and know that God will see us through. Then we can smile and say, 'It came to pass.' "

"And it came to pass" reminds me of 1 Peter 5:10, "And the God of all grace, who called you to his eternal glory in Christ, after you have suffered a little while, will himself restore you." I don't face drought and failing crops, but I am in a wheelchair; it's why I appreciate the words, "After you have suffered for a little while." Our troubles are but momentary according to 2 Corinthians 4:17, and very soon hardships will be behind us. What hardship are you facing? Thank the Lord that you'll soon say, "It came to pass."

Lord, keep me from a complaining spirit. Give me the courage to trust you no matter what I lack in life.

DAY 54

The Question of Good

All of us have become like one who is unclean, and all our righteous acts are like filthy rags; we all shrivel up like a leaf, and like the wind our sins sweep us away.

—Isaiah 64:6

This world is full of pain. People look at the anguish of those who hurt and insist, "Good people deserve better." But do we? It's a tough question, and the Bible has a hard answer. It paints a sobering picture: People are *not* innately good. It also says that people—all of us—cannot begin to comprehend how our sin has offended God. In fact, the Bible states that God is just to send rebellious creatures to hell. Thus, as incomprehensible as it may sound, he is fair to start that hell in this life.

But wait; there is a hidden mercy here! By tasting suffering in this life—hell's splash over—people are driven to ponder what may face them in the next life. In this way, suffering may be our greatest mercy; for many, suffering becomes God's roadblock on their headlong rush to hell. If we experienced nothing but ease and comfort, we would soon forget that we are eternal creatures—but suffering won't allow that. It persistently reminds us that something immense and cosmic is at stake—a heaven to be reached for Christ's sake, and a hell to be avoided.

Every day of our short life has eternal consequences for good or ill. Thus, it is only fitting that a merciful and wise God should give us some sense of the stakes involved, some sense of the magnitude of the spiritual battle. He does this by giving us foretastes of heaven in the joys we experience, and foretastes of hell in our suffering.

Open my eyes, Father, so that I might grasp how holy you are. Help me to see how cosmic and grand the eternal stakes really are in this life. And then, help me to live circumspectly and wisely!

DAY 55

The Good Answer

For God so loved the world that he gave his one and only Son, that whoever believes in him shall not perish but have eternal life. For God did not send his Son into the world to condemn the world, but to save the world through him. Whoever believes in him is not condemned, but whoever does not believe stands condemned already because they have not believed in the name of God's one and only Son.

—JOHN 3:16–18

If God is so good, why doesn't he get rid of the awful suffering in the world?! If God were to get rid of suffering, he would get rid of sinners—suffering is one of the consequences of our rebellion against God back in the garden. God does not want to obliterate sinners; he wants to save them (2 Peter 3:9).

The kingdom of heaven came to earth with the arrival of King

Jesus. When Christ died, God opened the way for sinners to be rescued. God was wise, however, in not finishing the kingdom when Christ was on earth. If he had closed the curtain on suffering, doing away with all pain and heartache, what would have become of us? God is rich in mercy toward us! He is delaying closing the curtain on sin and suffering so that more people—millions more over the last two thousand years—might come to know Christ.

And I promise you—the Bible promises you—five minutes of heaven will be worth the pain. Until then, our sufferings drive us to reach out toward unbelieving friends and neighbors with the good news that God so loved the world, that he gave his only begotten Son that whoever should believe on him should not perish, but have eternal life. The cost of suffering may be great, but people's souls are worth it.

Lord, I believe the eternal state of my neighbors and coworkers is worth the suffering I face in this world. Give boldness as I share John 3:16 today.

DAY 56

Reasons!

In all this you greatly rejoice, though now for a little while you may have had to suffer grief in all kinds of trials. These have come so that the proven genuineness of your faith—of greater worth than gold, which perishes even though refined by fire—may result in praise, glory and honor when Jesus Christ is revealed.

—1 PETER 1:6–7

Somewhere after my first decade in my wheelchair, I was gratified by the changes in my life. All things were working together for my good and God's glory—it didn't mean being an author or speaker; it meant being like Christ. Hardships were forcing me to make decisions about God—my faith was becoming more muscular. Suffering was doing a job on my character—I was able to stick to promises, not be sloppy in relationships, quit whining, and be more patient. My thoughts were being jerked right side up—I couldn't reach for the common temptations like before (having no hands helped with that). Also . . .

Suffering was making me more sensitive to others. I couldn't have cared less about people like me before my accident, but now it was a different story. Being paralyzed was making heaven come alive—not in a cop-out way, but in a way that made me want to live better here on earth because greater things were coming in the next life.

A checklist like this sounds dry and technical, but years ago it helped answer—at least in part—that sticky question, "Why does God pile on hardships so high?" Well—hey!—God is more concerned with conforming us to the likeness of his Son than leaving us in our comfort zones. God is more interested in inward qualities than outward circumstances. Today, look for the "reasons" God has for your hardship. When you find them, you will "move beyond the elementary teachings about Christ and be taken forward to maturity" (Hebrews 6:1).

Lord, you are the One who holds all the reasons in your hands. I can trust you with every reason!

DAY 57

And Reasons Lead to . . .

Yet for us there is but one God, the Father, from whom all things came and for whom we live; and there is but one Lord, Jesus Christ, through whom all things came and through whom we live.

—1 CORINTHIANS 8:6

Suffering is not pointless. God intends that our afflictions will lead to Christian maturity. God uses hardships to improve our character, remove sinful habits, make us heaven-hearted, and instill compassion toward others, to name a few.

But answers and reasons, no matter how good and true they are, cannot be the coup de grâce. Purified faith should never be an end in itself—it should culminate in God. Stronger character is made muscular not for its own sake, but God's. A livelier hope is more spirited because its focus is not on "things getting better," but on God. To forget this is to tarnish faith, weaken character, and deflate hope. As the Phillips' paraphrase puts 2 Peter 1:8, "If you have these qualities existing and growing in you then it means that *knowing our Lord Jesus Christ* has not made your lives either complacent or unproductive." It really is all about Jesus. Simply Jesus. "There is but one Lord, Jesus Christ, through whom we live."

We must never distance the Bible's reasons from God. The problem of suffering is not about some *thing*, but *Someone*. It follows that the answers and reasons must not be some thing, but Someone. The Bible never bids us to keep our eyes on suffering, or even suffering's benefits. Only on God, the One who wrote the book on suffering. Consider the good and valued benefits for the hardship in your life. Can you say with the apostle Paul, "I consider them garbage, that I may gain Christ and be found in him" (Philippians 3:8–9)?

> Lord Jesus, keep my focus off not only my hardships, but even whatever benefits might come of those hardships. May my focus always and only be on you. Especially today.

DAY 58

Behind-the-Scenes Miracles

Because you have seen me, you have believed; blessed are those who have not seen and yet have believed.

—John 20:29

Many Christians don't see God in their trials. If no miracles are happening—if the floods aren't receding or the cancer is not in remission—God must not be at work. We think of miracles as the kind we witnessed in the movie *The Ten Commandments*. "Those ten plagues on Egypt, now that was God up to something." Agreed, frogs and lice in Pharaoh's bed made for a great film years ago. Ah, but if we could only watch the real movie of how God runs the world from behind the scenes . . .

Oh, the infinite complexity of it all! The wrenching of good out of evil like blood from a turnip; the clandestine exploiting of Satan's worst escapades; the balancing act of weather systems across the globe that assure the arrival of summer; the infiltration of grace and salvation behind even the barbwire of Russian death camps; the exact number of white blood cells called into action to defeat your illness—*that* will win an Oscar. The delicately balanced, invisible workings of our great God—this is real drama. Meanwhile, he wants us to trust him. As Jesus told skeptical Thomas after the resurrection, "Blessed are those who have not seen and yet have believed."

So why do we still doubt? Perhaps we cannot find wrapping paper wide enough to package these truths neatly. No one can grasp the Almighty and his miracles. "Even angels long to look into these things" (1 Peter 1:12). However, our inability to comprehend something doesn't make it untrue or any less miraculous. As Paul put it, "How unsearchable his judgments, and his paths beyond tracing out!" (Romans 11:33). Count his miracles today . . . and thank him.

Lord, thank you for every miracle today, whether it is to heal or spread encouragement, or to defeat the works of darkness. I believe!

DAY 59

Living Under the Curse

But he was pierced for our transgressions, he was crushed for our iniquities; the punishment that brought us peace was on him, and by his wounds we are healed.

—Isaiah 53:5

It is true that disease flows from the curse God pronounced on us after Adam's rebellion. It is also true that Jesus came to reverse this curse. But does this mean Christians shouldn't have to put up with cancer, Down syndrome, Lyme disease, or Alzheimer's? We'd like to think that since Jesus came to take up our diseases, there should be healing for everything from migraines to menopausal sweats. But that's akin to saying, "There's an oak in every acorn—so take this acorn and start sawing planks for picnic tables." Or it's like saying, "Congress just passed a Clean Water Act, so tomorrow morning Manhattan residents can start drinking from the East River." Forty years will pass before that oak is ready for lumbering. Purging industrial ooze out of a river will take decades.

And so it is with Jesus' reversal of sin's curse (and the suffering that goes with it). What Jesus began doing to sin and its results won't be complete until the second coming. The purchase of salvation was complete, and the outcome was settled with certainty. But the application of salvation to God's people was anything but finished. God "*has* saved" us, yet we are still "being saved" (1 Corinthians 1:18). We are still on earth; this means we're still going to feel the influence of that old curse. At least until heaven!

First Corinthians 15:45 calls Jesus "the last Adam" who came to undo the curse triggered in the garden of Eden—but this summer you'll still be wrestling with weeds in your backyard, as well as a backache from all that hoeing. Only in paradise will it be said, "No longer will there be any curse" (Revelation 22:3).

Jesus, thank you that you saved me . . . and that I am still being saved. I look to that day in heaven when there will be no more sorrow, sickness, disease, or death!

DAY 60

He Carried Our Sorrows

Surely he took up our pain and bore our suffering . . .
—Isaiah 53:4

Nobody likes to be sad. No Christian welcomes grief. So aren't you glad that Jesus carried our sorrows when he went to the cross?! But sorrow did not cease with the death and resurrection of Christ. Think of the apostle Paul who confessed to "great sorrow and unceasing anguish in my heart" over the spiritual lostness of his race. He also described Christ's apostles as "*sorrowful*, yet always rejoicing." Jesus' death did not hinder him from saying, "Blessed are you who weep now." It did not hinder James from advising us to "grieve, mourn and wail" when we sin. Sorrow and tears, disappointment and grief are written into God's plan for you and me. To be sure, he lightens and brightens our days with glimpses of paradise; he ladles out foretastes of bliss through a thousand blessings large and small. But they are all just that—glimpses and foretastes. We are not in heaven yet. We are destined to experience earth's sorrow.

But when tears and sorrow come, we look to Jesus—he bore to the cross the very tears you cry. He blamed no one when he felt the weight of grief and disappointment. He did not shrink from sorrow, nor sink under the burden of sadness. The load was heavy and the way was long, but he persevered. *And he gives you power to do the same.*

When we grieve and feel deep sorrow, we must look to Jesus, who endured a greater grief and sorrow. There's a reason Jesus says, "Blessed are those who mourn." Sorrow forces you and me to identify more deeply with the Savior when he carried his cross. If you are experiencing sorrow, if your tears seem to flow endlessly over a deep disappointment, remember the Savior. He persevered. That means you can too.

When I grieve, thank you, Lord God, for supporting me with your presence and consolation. My tears help me to know you better. They drive me into your comforting arms. Thank you for that.

DAY 61

A Good Kind of Anger

You have put me in the lowest pit, in the darkest depths. Your wrath lies heavily on me; you have overwhelmed me with all your waves. . . . But I cry to you for help, Lord; in the morning my prayer comes before you. Why, Lord, do you reject me and hide your face from me?

—Psalm 88:6–7, 13–14

The author of Psalm 88 doesn't complain *about* God, but he sure does complain *to* God. He abruptly stops his psalm on a note of resentment. No setup for a hopeful ending. No hand-is-quicker-than-the-eye move from moaning to praise. Not even a sniff of joy in the entire eighteen verses. God seems snide and cruel, smashing underfoot helpless humans as though they were cigarette butts. The words are ugly. Then again, so is life.

God is big enough to take on anger. He knows stuff happens.

He said, "In this world you will have trouble." He does not tiptoe around ugly things, embarrassed at wit's end to explain our woes. He doesn't cover up the guts of a person's rage—he invited people like the one who wrote Psalm 88 to be his coauthors. In so doing, he invited frustrated, angry people to air their complaints.

Too often we choose the polite routine and repress our deep emotions toward God. But anger pushes the problem to the front burner. Strong emotions open the door to asking the really hard questions: Does life make sense? Is God good? Anger often reveals whether we are moving toward the Almighty or away from him.

Take your complaints to God. Like the psalmist, move toward him, not away from him. Don't sow seeds of discord or incite rebellion among your friends against God, but allow your hurt to engage him head-on. This makes anger a good kind of anger. It's the point behind Ephesians 4:26, "In your anger do not sin."

Lord, may my anger drive me into your arms. Help me to point my anger, frustration, and bewilderment Godward.

Take your
complaints to God.
Like the psalmist,
move toward him,
not away from him.

DAY 62

My Own Baggage

But when they measure themselves by one another, and compare themselves with one another, they are without understanding.

—2 CORINTHIANS 10:12 RSV

I have been at countless airport luggage carousels, watching as innumerable bags drop from the chute. Some of those pieces are very nice. Smart leather trim. Clean. New. In my daydreams I wonder what would happen if I swapped my old, scuffed-up luggage for one of those fancy new pieces? I wouldn't, of course. But *if* I did, what might I find inside? Elegant clothes that don't fit. Shoes I don't like. Makeup that doesn't match my skin tone. Jewelry that's clunky and overdone. And what might I *lose* in this hypothetical deal? I'd lose my speaking notes, my favorite dress jeans, and treasured personal jewelry. I would lose the devotional book I love to read in the morning. In fact, while the bag I took might look better on the *outside*, it's a no-brainer that the stuff on the *inside* wouldn't be a good fit at all.

Sometimes we like to imagine ourselves swapping lives with others—lives that look so much more attractive and desirable than our own. But the truth is, we really don't know what's *inside* their lives. We forget that God has equipped and enabled us with special abilities to cope, grow, and thrive through life's challenges. We forget the loyal friends and wonderful people he has placed around us, and we forget the incomparable, eternal purposes he is working through our lives. I may have difficulties in my life because of my disability, but I wouldn't trade my "baggage" for anyone else's!

Sometimes when we long to escape the life we have, it's because we have failed to take stock of our blessings and resources. Think through the friendships, life experiences, encouragement from other believers, and gracious provisions from the Lord that are part of your "baggage" today.

Father God, I thank you for the unique way you have provided for me, showing me your tender love through the years. Help me to keep my eyes focused on Jesus, rather than comparing myself to others.

DAY 63

Steering Sin

The Lord *works out everything to its proper end—even the wicked for a day of disaster.*

—Proverbs 16:4

God is a lot bigger than we think. A whole lot bigger. Most Christians willingly acknowledge God's hand in people's good deeds, even the good deeds of serious atheists. But God also oversees people's wicked actions. No sin happens that God doesn't deliberately allow. (A statement like that will take your breath away!) Don't misunderstand—he is not the source of people's bad deeds, for he despises sin. He hates it. James 1:13 says that God never tempts anyone to do wrong. Nevertheless, his overarching decrees allow for God to turn wicked hearts and evil motives this way and that, all to suit his higher purpose. It's what Proverbs 16:4 is all about.

So how does our big God pull it off? He steers the sin *already in people's hearts* so that sinners unwittingly fulfill God's plans and not merely their own. Look at wicked King Ahab of Israel. As he was mustering his troops for war, a courageous prophet tells him what he does not want to hear: "The Lord has decreed disaster for you." Decreed, mind you—Ahab's death in battle is not a suggestion-box item that God is merely considering. Jehovah plotted Ahab's demise. And even when the wicked king tried to cleverly subvert God's decree, he still ended up dying in battle (2 Chronicles 18:33–34). How did God *do* that?! He accomplished it, and countless similar circumstances, by infinite wisdom far beyond our grasp.

Little wonder God's Word tells us to cultivate a fear of the Lord (Psalm 111:10; Proverbs 1:7). A proper fear begins with understanding how big God really is. Reread this devotional with that in mind.

Lord God, there is no way I can understand the way you do things. I don't pretend to comprehend how you work through people's evil deeds to serve your own ends. But I know this: I believe you are far more kind and gracious than I could possibly imagine.

DAY 64

Fruit Comes Through Struggle

This is to my Father's glory, that you bear much fruit, showing yourselves to be my disciples.

—John 15:8

Last week Ken and I visited Tim, a friend from church, who grows several rare varieties of grapes on the hillside behind his house. I was surprised that Tim had planted his vines along a steep and rocky portion of the hill. "Why didn't you plant the vines at the base of the hill?" I asked him. "The soil certainly looks a lot better—and there's more sun."

Tim smiled. "There's a rule you need to remember when it comes to growing these special varieties of grapes," he said. "When you feed them luxuriously with lots of nutrients and fertilizer, the vine produces a profuse bush of leaves and cane. But the fruit it grows is sparse and very poor. Oh, make no mistake," he laughed, "the plant *loves* lots of fertilizer. But it invests all those nutrients into growing lush, dark, beautiful leaves. And when the vine has finished doing that, it has very little energy left to produce fruit. It certainly looks like a beautiful vine. But that's it. It just looks good."

How, then, do you get good grapes? As Tim explained it, you have to make sure the grapevine struggles! You plant it in rocky, flinty soil, or you girdle the vine by wrapping wires around the cordons, forcing the plant to struggle as it tries to draw nutrients from its roots. This causes the distressed vine to divert most all of its prized and hard-won nutrients into the fruit, instead of the leaves. The result of these trials and tribulations is the sweetest fruit possible!

So . . . maybe the rocky soil and steep inclines in your life aren't so bad after all. The trials and struggles, disappointments and setbacks you face, this "girdling" that presses you in from all sides . . . is a bruising of blessing. And you won't bear a crop without it.

Lord, when this life is all over and I stand before you, I want you to find sweet fruit in my life and not just leaves.

DAY 65

Job's Trials

Then the Lord *said to Satan, "Have you considered my servant Job?"*

—Job 1:8

The Bible infers that God always eventually gets his way. But what does that say about him? God's favorite planet has experienced a lot of evil over the years. Why hasn't he stopped it . . . or at least curbed it? If God's the boss, is Satan his employee? Let's look at Job.

Job had it all—money, land, status, family. One day in God's throne room, Satan broached his disgust over Job's pious reputation. "The man loves you because you bribe him," the devil argued. "But stretch out your hand and strike everything he has, and he will surely curse you to your face." God answered, "Job is yours, only don't lay a finger on his person." The words were scarcely out of God's mouth when lightning killed Job's sheep and shepherds, a Chaldean raiding party plundered the cattle and herdsmen, then a mighty wind collapsed a roof on Job's children. So we ask, who caused Job's trials?

At the most basic level, *natural forces* did—desert winds blew and lightning struck. On the same level, *evil people* caused Job's trials—greedy men killed and plundered. On another level, *Satan* caused Job's problems—he leaves God's presence, we scarcely blink, and carnage is everywhere; Satan engineered it all: the fire, the wind, and the sword. But on the deepest level, *nothing happened that God did not decree*. God permitted what he hated, to accomplish something he loved: the worship of a wiser Job.

Satan's motive was to wreck Job's life and mock God. God's reaction to the devil was merely to lengthen his leash. God's decree made room for evil to occur, but God didn't *do* it. He simply exploited the deliberate evil of wicked people, as well as the impersonal evil of some bad storms *without forcing anyone's hands*. How does God pull it off? Welcome to the world of finite human beings trying to comprehend an infinite God!

Almighty God, how unsearchable are your judgments and your ways past finding out! I simply praise you that your decrees are perfect.

DAY 66

Prepare to Meet Your God

I know that everything God does will endure forever; nothing can be added to it and nothing taken from it. God does it so that people will fear him. Whatever is has already been, and what will be has been before; and God will call the past to account.

— Ecclesiastes 3:14–15

Don't be afraid of this verse. It's good news! God will one day call your past into account, and he will no doubt see smudges and stains, sins and faults. He will also see the blood of his Son, which will cover all (Hebrews 9:14). What else about your past? God will see countless times of obedience and perseverance, trust and confidence in him; he will recognize your doggedness through hardship and your resolve against temptation. Again, it will be his Son who made the provision of grace upon grace. When God calls everything about you into account, you will praise God for the blood and the blessings of Jesus as never before!

You will drop to your knees before Jesus to express thanks and gratitude. The Man of Sorrows will walk from his throne and approach you. He will have absolutely no doubt of your appreciation, for he knows what you have suffered, what you have endured, the temptations to which you said no. He will reach toward you with his nail-scarred hands, and when you feel your hands in his, you will not be embarrassed. That's because your own scars, and all those times you felt rejection and pain, have given you at least a tiny taste of what the Savior endured to purchase your redemption.

Your hardships, like nothing else, are preparing you to meet your God. Your suffering is getting you ready—for what proof could you bring of your love for Jesus if this life left you totally un-scarred?

Gracious God, I am full of praise for Jesus Christ. His blood covers my sins, and his blessings of grace help me live righteously. He deserves all the praise!

DAY 67

The Exaltation of Christ

Therefore God exalted him to the highest place and gave him the name that is above every name, that at the name of Jesus every knee should bow, in heaven and on earth and under the earth, and every tongue acknowledge that Jesus Christ is Lord, to the glory of God the Father.

—PHILIPPIANS 2:9–11

I can't wait for the day described in our verse. It will be a glorious, grand day for Jesus! Christ's status as the God-man means that the Father will give his Son privileges he did not have prior to the incarnation. He will be crowned King of kings and Lord of lords. He will receive back his glory because he crushed the adversary. He will be honored for having rescued sinful man by his own sacrifice. "Jesus" was the name bestowed at his birth, but "Lord" is what *everyone* will call him after his exaltation.

When every knee finally bows and every tongue confesses that Jesus Christ is Lord, we will confess him as the undisputed Sovereign Ruler of the universe. These confessions will not only come from the saints and angels but from the demons and lost humanity in hell—*everyone* will eventually agree that Jesus is Lord. They will do so willfully and happily, or unwillfully and painfully. But they'll do it. Not everyone will be saved, but everyone will acknowledge Jesus as the rightful Ruler of the universe, never to be contested again. What a glorious day that will be!

You can begin practicing for the wonderful "day of Christ," a day described three times in the book of Philippians—a day of rewards for believers, final salvation, and glorification. But remember, it's Jesus' day. You will be among those who willfully and happily bow the knee to confess that Jesus is Lord!

Father, thank you for all the privileges and honors you will bestow upon your Son on that awesome day. May I bow my knee in submission to him even now while I'm on earth.

DAY 68

The God of Hope

May the God of hope fill you with all joy and peace as you trust in him, so that you may overflow with hope by the power of the Holy Spirit.

—ROMANS 15:13

I was on the phone an hour with Ron. His wife had contacted me, distraught that he was depressed and had been lying in bed since he broke his neck. Ron was a former pastor and probably knew more Scripture than I did. When he didn't respond after an hour, I took a different tack. "Did you see the movie *The Shawshank Redemption*?" He seemed surprised at my question. "Remember when Andy Dufresne said to his fellow prisoner, 'Hope is a good thing, maybe the best of things, and no good thing ever dies . . . so get busy living, or get busy dying.' "[9] Ron was quiet for a long moment then said softly, "Hope *is* a good thing." From then on, he got busy living.

It's amazing how far we can go on a little bit of hope. Hope means "I know I can make it!" The source of all hope is none other than Jesus Christ. Titus 2:13 (KJV) says, "Looking for that blessed hope, and the glorious appearing of the great God and our Saviour Jesus Christ." No wonder Paul tells us to trust in "the God of hope." From the Lord alone flows all joy and peace. I saw hope overflow in Ron's life when he and his wife finally came to one of our Family Retreats. There they were, passing on hope to others!

Hope happens when we gently point people to Jesus, whether through a few encouraging words, a Scripture in a note card, or just spending an hour on the phone together. Today, nudge people toward "the Blessed Hope," the Lord Jesus.

Father, because you are the God of Hope, I have assurance that I can make it through the toughest of times. Help me to pass on your hope to a hurting friend today.

DAY 69

Waiting in Prayer

In the morning, Lord, you hear my voice; in the morning
I lay my requests before you and wait expectantly.

—Psalm 5:3

When our Wheels for the World team was in Peru, we met Angelica Ramirez, a twenty-five-year-old woman who had cerebral palsy and epilepsy since birth. For most of her life, she had lain in bed all day—her only entertainment was watching the shaft of the sun move across her room. On the morning of our wheelchair distribution, Angelica's mother wrapped her daughter in a white mattress pad so that her brother could carry her down the mountain. They were hoping to receive a wheelchair.

Our team happened to have a recliner wheelchair with an extended headrest (we don't usually take these sorts of highly customized chairs on trips). As Angelica was placed in this particular chair, everyone gasped. It fit perfectly. When our team gave Angelica's mother a Bible in the Spanish language, she broke down and began sobbing. "God has answered my prayer," she said through an interpreter. We smiled, thinking she meant the Bible. But the woman shook her head and explained, "I want you to understand that I have been praying for twenty years for a wheelchair for my daughter and today—*Gloria al Dios*—God has answered my plea. Now I can take my daughter to church. I won't have to worry about carrying her!"

If God answers your prayer immediately, be thankful; if it's denied, be patient; if you are to wait, remain eager and expectant. Angelica's story taught me something fresh about laying our requests before God: He invites us to have an expectant attitude when we pray. He wants us to be hopeful and eager—even if the answer is delayed for twenty years! Why such a delay? Only God knows, but I know this: He provided a perfect wheelchair hand tailored for Angelica, and that Peruvian mother experienced twenty times the joy.

Thank you for hearing my voice in prayer, O Lord. I trust you with the answer and I wait eagerly—not impatiently—for your reply.

DAY 70

It Could Be Worse

The eternal God is your refuge, and
underneath are the everlasting arms.
—Deuteronomy 33:27

You've heard that old cliché, "It could be worse!" It's not a phrase we like to hear. The words can sound rather trite and empty at times. But it's *true*. Things truly could be much worse for all of us. Picture God holding up his hands like the flood-control locks on a canal, holding back a dark tidal wave of suffering and harm. His everlasting arms shield us. He is our refuge and protector. Were it not for the influence of the Spirit of Christ in this world, we would see much more calamity, violence, natural catastrophes, war, and crime. Most of all, thank God we don't get the sentence of death we deserve for our sins, but rather the rescue and salvation he so freely offered to us in his Son!

Are you experiencing hardship today? God promises that absolutely nothing will penetrate his sheltering hands to touch us except that which has been weighed and measured, so as to not ultimately harm us. And when troubles do encroach on our lives, God promises to flood us with his sustaining grace.

And though our world can be a dark and sorrowful place at times, we can still experience our Father's goodness in the simple pleasures of a rainbow burning against a dark sky, a honeybee exploring a daffodil, the soft morning sunlight, a cup of cocoa by a cherrywood fire on a stormy night, the whisper of a summer wind in the pines, the companionship of a loved one, and the hope of a wondrous new dawn in our heavenly home, just around the corner.

Take a moment to think through the good in your life—the things and the people you love and value. Then spend some time thanking the one who sends us "every good and perfect gift" (James 1:17).

Bless you, my Father, for your guarding and shielding me from so much evil, so much harm and grief. Grant me a grateful, thankful heart through the hours of this day.

God promises that absolutely nothing will penetrate his sheltering hands to touch us except that which has been weighed and measured, so as to not ultimately harm us.

DAY 71

God Meant It for Good

But God sent me ahead of you to preserve for you a remnant on earth and to save your lives by a great deliverance. So then, it was not you who sent me here, but God. He made me father to Pharaoh, lord of his entire household and ruler of all Egypt.

—GENESIS 45:7–8

Whenever I become troubled by crazy things that happen to me, I turn to the story of Joseph in the Bible. *There* was somebody who *really* went through bizarre circumstances! But think about it. If Joseph had not been sold to those caravan traders by his wicked brothers, he would not have been sold as a slave to Pharaoh. And if Joseph had not become Pharaoh's right-hand man, no one would have thought to build giant grain silos to ward off the seven-year famine. And if the famine hadn't happened, Jacob and his family would never have come to Egypt for food and safety. And if Jacob's family weren't in Egypt, there would have been no slave laborers. And if no slaves, no exodus. And no Mount Sinai and the giving of the law to Moses. And no Promised Land. And, finally, no line of Judah from which the Messiah, Jesus Christ, would come.

It is enthralling to see how the troubles of one young man named Joseph could kick-start a whole chain of earthshaking events that would ultimately lead to our salvation. Oh, the wisdom and knowledge of God!

Joseph's story could be yours. Only heaven will reveal the incredibly complex intertwining of events in which you have played a pivotal role. Like Joseph, you may not be able to discern it at the time, but God has it all in hand . . . he has it all in control . . . and you, dear friend, are needed in his marvelous plan to spread his kingdom in your corner of the world.

God of Abraham, Isaac, and Jacob, thank you for the awe-inspiring lessons about your sovereignty that you teach us through the story of Joseph. Thank you for your dominion and rule, not only in his life, but mine.

DAY 72

The Price of Identifying

Since the children have flesh and blood,
he too shared in their humanity.
—Hebrews 2:14

When we are hurting, if there is one thing that eases our pain or grief, it is this: We want someone to *understand*. We want somebody to really identify with us, to have some idea of what we're enduring.

It is certainly like that for me. I hate feeling alone and alienated in those dark times when my paralysis seems overwhelming. On my really rough days it helps to remember what the Bible tells us about Jesus identifying with us in our sufferings. It says that he was tested and tried in every way like us. That helps! When it comes to suffering, the Lord Jesus has gone ahead of us and has intimate, experiential, firsthand knowledge of the pain, the weight, the frustration, and the struggle. He appreciates. He understands. He connects.

But it works both ways! Not only does Christ identify with us in our suffering, we identify with him in *his* suffering. He identifies with us, and we identify with him. He appreciates all that it means to be human, and we appreciate all that his divine grace supplies. Through suffering, he participates in our humanity; through suffering, we participate in his divinity.

So why do we struggle so to escape our suffering? Why do we look so desperately for release? I suppose this is why I'm not earnestly seeking to be healed and raised up out of this wheelchair. I see this trial of mine as a window into the heart of Jesus. Suffering is a connecting point between my Savior and me. And when I see his great love on the cross, it gives me courage to take up my cross and follow him.

Do you want someone to understand what you are going through today? Turn to Jesus. When you do, you will better understand what he has gone through for you.

Lord Jesus, sometimes in my grief or suffering I just want to run away and hide. Help me, Savior, to run away to you and to hide in you.

DAY 73

When Pain Moves In

My back is filled with searing pain; there is no health in my body. I am feeble and utterly crushed; I groan in anguish of heart . . . LORD, I wait for you; you will answer, Lord my God.

—PSALM 38:7–8, 15

The realization may have been years in the making, or it may have come in one swift, devastating stroke. But at last you know that pain—your pain, whatever it may be—is here to stay. Perhaps it is an illness, a rebellious child, a chronic muscle problem, the death of a loved one, or a severe disability in the family. Whatever form it takes, it's the common experience of all people. Human pain wears a thousand guises.

After five decades of permanent paralysis, I can attest that only a daily, hourly, even momentary placing of our throbbing into God's strong hands can protect us from the crippling ravages of fear. There are countless "fear nots" in Scripture, each one of them covering the whole spectrum of human experience. Every "fear not" can be embraced and impressed on our hearts and repeated in the presence of our adversary. Then we will press to our hearts this poem by Miss Margaret Clarkson, a woman who was bedridden for years with chronic pain:

> Lord Jesus, King of pain,
> Thy subject I; Thy right it is to reign:
> Oh, hear my cry, and bid in me all longings cease;
> save for Thy holy will's increase.
> Thy right it is to reign o'er all Thine own;
> then, if Thy love send pain, find there Thy throne,
> and help me bear it unto Thee,
> who didst bear death and hell for me.
> Lord Jesus, King of pain, my heart's adored,
> teach me eternal gain is love's reward:
> in Thee I hide me; hold me still
> till pain work all Thy perfect will.[10]

When I struggle with pain, dear Lord, teach me to wait on thee and remember the example of Jesus, the King of Pain.

DAY 74

The Lord's Right Hand

In his right hand he held seven stars, and coming out of his mouth was a sharp, double-edged sword. His face was like the sun shining in all its brilliance. When I saw him, I fell at his feet as though dead. Then he placed his right hand on me and said: "Do not be afraid. I am the First and the Last."

—Revelation 1:16–17

Every year I plunge into the book of Revelation (daunting as it may be), asking God to show me something fresh about himself. Well, this year, he answered my prayer in the very first chapter. Beginning in verse 12, the apostle John describes a stunning vision of the resurrected Christ. I stopped my reading here and tried hard to visualize the actual moment. I saw Jesus, the Ancient of Days, the First and the Last, standing there holding seven stars in his right hand. And not just any stars—these represent the seven angels of the seven churches. Now, here's what amazes me. When John is overcome by the vision (and who wouldn't be?) he falls at Jesus' feet, nearly frightened to death. The text says that the Lord takes his right hand—the hand still holding up the stars and the churches (he doesn't let them go or set them down)—and gently bends down to touch and comfort John.

This is astonishing! Our Savior stoops to give us his right hand, not the left, but his righteous right hand. This is the same hand that keeps stars and suns and planets spinning in motion, and the hand that upholds his church and its messengers all over the world.

Do you see it? Even though the Son of God is awesome in his glory and power, he does not think your needs—your hurts, your fears, your emotions—are beneath him. High and exalted as he now is, he still takes delight in bending low. His right hand may perform great and wondrous things beyond description, but he also reserves that same hand to gently touch you at your deepest point of need.

Lord, thank you for this picture of your majesty and your tenderness.

DAY 75

The Shiny, Sharp Tool

But Zerubbabel, Jeshua and the rest of the heads of the families of Israel answered, "You have no part with us in building a temple to our God. We alone will build it for the Lord, *the God of Israel. . . ." They bribed officials to work against them and frustrate their plans during the entire reign of Cyrus king of Persia and down to the reign of Darius king of Persia.*

—Ezra 4:3,5

Dorothy Williams was a British missionary who served in West Africa during the 1930s. She was a nurse from Wales and spent her time on the mission field training African nurses. This amazed her mission board back home—Dorothy was very frail; they didn't expect her to last but a year or two working in Africa! But with God's help, she refused to be discouraged by her limitations. This inspired the young African nurses under her charge who were often disheartened by their own poverty and lack of resources.

One day a young nurse was carrying a tray of surgical instruments, and Dorothy noticed a sad look in her student's eyes. "Oh, Mum, I am feeling much afraid today," to which Dorothy replied, "Dearie, look at these shiny instruments on your tray." The British missionary picked up the pointiest one, then added, "The devil has a tray of instruments too, and the shiniest and sharpest is his tool of discouragement—it's sharp because he uses it so often." The student nurse smiled, blushed, and then went on her way with fresh resolve.

Ezra 4:4 describes the devil's strategy against God's people. It is "to discourage the people . . . and make them afraid . . . to work against them and frustrate their plans." Do not be fearful, for the Bible repeats 112 times, "Do not be afraid." And Dorothy would add, "Don't be discouraged." You have your own shiny, sharp tool: the Word of God (Hebrews 4:12). Keep it sharp and use it often against your adversary!

God of all encouragement, thank you that I never have a reason to be afraid!

DAY 76

What Do I Have?

I am not saying this because I am in need, for I have learned to be content whatever the circumstances. I know what it is to be in need, and I know what it is to have plenty. I have learned the secret of being content in any and every situation, whether well fed or hungry, whether living in plenty or in want.

—PHILIPPIANS 4:11–12

"*All I need, I already have*." Do you believe that statement? It is one I have wrestled with in recent days. *What do I have?* Well, I *don't* have use of my hands, legs, or the sense of touch to feel Ken's embrace. But I do have a voice, a wheelchair, and a husband who loves me. And that, according to the Lord, is all I need. For if there was anything more I needed, he would have given it to me. *Am I using what I have?* God never gives us a task without supplying the need. His command never comes without empowerment. *Am I prepared to lose what I have?* This is the litmus test of contentment. Despite Job's agony, he declared, "Though he slay me, yet will I hope in him" (Job 13:15). He was prepared to believe, even to the point of death. To be honest, when I think of the future, I sometimes get scared. I know my good health won't last forever. But my calling is not only to abandon my future wants, but to trust in God and hand over what I already possess. *Am I ready to receive what I do not have?* Well, my friend, it's not as though I'm looking to "enlarge my borders" like Jabez and expand my spiritual territory. I'd just be happy if God would simply make my *heart* larger, to receive more of his peace and joy.

All you need, you already have. What do you have? How long has it been since you did a thoughtful inventory of your possessions? The secret of contentment is wrapped up in simple gratitude for what God has already provided you.

Father, I'm so often like the ungrateful Israelites, who even complained about the sweet, nourishing "bread of angels" that appeared at their feet each morning. Forgive me for looking down on your "manna" in my life, and hankering after more exotic fare.

DAY 77

Therefore . . .

In your relationships with one another, have the same mindset as Christ Jesus: Who, being in very nature God, did not consider equality with God something to be used to his own advantage; rather, he made himself nothing by taking the very nature of a servant, being made in human likeness. And being found in appearance as a man, he humbled himself by becoming obedient to death—even death on a cross! Therefore God exalted him to the highest place and gave him the name that is above every name.

—PHILIPPIANS 2:5–9

Notice the "therefore" in today's reading. Jesus was on a journey of humility—he was God, but he made himself nothing. He was a servant, and he was utterly obedient, even unto death. And not only an average death, but death on the cross. At each level, Jesus humbles himself more. And the point? "Your attitude should be the same as that of Christ Jesus." You may be a "somebody," but God would have you make yourself a "nobody" in the world's eyes. But does it end there?

No! *Therefore* God exalted Jesus . . . and God will exalt you to be a co-heir with Christ. "We are heirs—heirs of God and co-heirs with Christ, if indeed we share in his sufferings in order that we may also share in his glory" (Romans 8:17). It's like a math formula or an inverse proportion. The more we humble ourselves, the more God will raise us up not to just any old high place but as a co-heir seated alongside our Savior. Astounding! We suffer with Christ—that we may share in Christ's *highest glory*. Believers who face the greatest conflict, yet hold on to God with all their hearts—these are the ones who have the greatest confidence in sharing Christ's glory.

In what way can you humble yourself today? Is an apology owed to a friend or a family member? Is there an elderly person in your apartment unit you can help with a chore? Can you volunteer as a teacher's aide in the special needs class at church?

I humble myself today in the sight of you, O Lord.

DAY 78

Eyes . . . Blind or Open?

"You will not certainly die," the serpent said to the woman. "For God knows that when you eat from it your eyes will be opened, and you will be like God, knowing good and evil."

—Genesis 3:4–5

The devil will promise you one thing but always deliver something opposite. Take the promise he gave Eve that her eyes would be opened. Inferring that she was somehow blind to really great spiritual things, the devil promised he could open her eyes. He promised she would become spiritually wise, knowing the secrets of heaven, and even the loftiest thoughts of God himself. That was the promise. But it was a lie.

The exact opposite happened when Eve believed the devil. Second Corinthians 4:4–5 says, "The god of this age has blinded the minds of unbelievers, so that they cannot see the light that displays the gospel of the glory of Christ, who is the image of God." People who do not know Christ cannot see his light. The adversary has blinded them.

God is the only one who can spiritually open our eyes. Acts 9:17–18 records the amazing story of Saul's spiritual eye surgery: "Placing his hands on Saul, [Ananias] said, 'Brother Saul, the Lord—Jesus, who appeared to you on the road as you were coming here—has sent me so that you may see again and be filled with the Holy Spirit.' Immediately, something like scales fell from Saul's eyes, and he could see again."

What promise has the devil whispered to you? How has he enticed you to compromise what you believe about God? What command from the Bible has the adversary told you is not necessary? Don't listen to him. "I pray that the eyes of your heart may be enlightened in order that you may know the hope to which he has called you" (Ephesians 1:18–19).

Lord God, I choose to listen to you, not the devil. The devil is a liar, but your promises are true. Thank you that Jesus is "the Truth and the Life."

DAY 79

When in Pain

Remember your word to your servant, for you have given me hope. My comfort in my suffering is this: Your promise preserves my life.

—Psalm 119:49–50

My heart goes out to people who suffer with physical pain. Oh, how hope is needed! Michael wrote, "Two years ago, tumors were pinching my sciatic nerve, and I was forced to my knees in tears. I couldn't stand the pain anymore. I shut myself in a room, lay on the floor, and shouted to the Lord, 'I am not leaving here until you do something. Kill me, heal me, but don't let me suffer like this!!!' It was a little later, and then I heard a still small voice, 'Peace I leave with you; my peace I give you. I do not give to you as the world gives. Do not let your hearts be troubled and do not be afraid'" (John 14:27).

Michael was encouraged by John 14:27 because when God gives

peace, he is imparting a sense of the presence of the Prince of Peace, his Son, Jesus. Michael can endure almost anything, as long as he knows Jesus is "lying on the floor" with him. And as Psalm 119:49 assures, God's comfort envelops Michael every time he remembers a promise like that from the Word.

I can identify. For me, when the pain doesn't go away, I'm quick to remember promises like John 14:27. My comfort in my suffering is this: The promise of God's presence *preserves* my life. Just knowing he's "with me" gives me peace, hope, and comfort. It sees me through.

Meditate on these verses in Psalm 119. Think of God's promises you know from Scripture. How do they preserve your life, especially when you are suffering physical or emotional pain?

Lord Jesus, thank you for giving me your peace when I hurt. Bless you for the hope and comfort I always find in you. Every single one of your promises preserves my life—I could not survive without your precious Word sustaining me every moment.

DAY 80

Quality and Quantity

A thief is only there to steal and kill and destroy. I came so they can have real and eternal life, more and better life than they ever dreamed of.

—John 10:10 The Message

Have you ever wondered why Jesus launched his public ministry by turning water into wine at a wedding party? I once heard my friend, Bible teacher Kay Arthur, describe this miracle as one of highest quality *and* quantity. "That," she exclaimed, "is the way Jesus does things."

Those six stone jars Jesus told the servants to fill with water were huge, each containing thirty gallons. And those servants filled each jar to the brim. Surely one—or possibly two—of those containers would have been plenty. But Jesus did six. And quality? This wasn't the plain label stuff they sell in a jug. The wine Jesus made was Gold

Medallion—probably ten grades above the best French vintage. The master of the banquet was astounded after he tasted the wine that only moments before had been common well water. "*You've saved the best for last!*" That's what Jesus chose to do. He gave much better than anyone expected.

Quality. Quantity. Not either/or, but both/and. That's what he wants to do in your life: "I have come that you may have life, and have it to the full." The life he is talking about, of course, is his very own life, flowing in and through you. This is life that spills over the brim. As the apostle says, you are a participator in the divine nature. You can't get any better than that!

The key to this life is in the counsel the Lord's mother gave to the servants that day. Mary said, "Do whatever he tells you." Follow that advice, my friend, and be prepared for his abundant life—lavish with quantity and radiant with quality.

Great God of grace, you didn't have to fill my life to overflowing ... and yet you did. You didn't have to share your character, your strength, and your joy with me ... and yet you have.

DAY 81

Crowded to Christ

In all this you greatly rejoice, though now for a little while you may have had to suffer grief in all kinds of trials. These have come so that the proven genuineness of your faith—of greater worth than gold, which perishes even though refined by fire—may result in praise, glory and honor when Jesus Christ is revealed.

—1 Peter 1:6–7

After a wartime marriage, Margie Hamilton's husband was killed. Then a little later her baby was born with a cruel deformity. After about forty operations, poverty followed. Still she said, "All this trouble has crowded me to Christ. It's simply mud around the gold."

I don't know who Margie Hamilton was, but this little story is as precious as gold. It's easy to run happily and willingly into God's arms, but I praise God for the trials and pain that literally crowd me to Christ. It's one reason I'm glad for this wheelchair. If I were on my feet, I'd either be checking out the sales or heading for the tennis court, coffee-klatching with too many girlfriends or flicking through daytime soaps. So I greatly rejoice in the "all kinds of trials" that accompany my wheelchair; it is headaches and hardships that thrust me flat on my face before the throne of grace where I find divine help (Hebrews 4:16). Sometimes the help God gives is an increased measure of faith—I am able to believe God more, as well as act on it. This is what makes faith golden!

I may feel weary and tired now, but one day the mud and dirt of my earthly heartaches will be washed away, revealing the gold of refined faith. Thank you for the reminder, Mrs. Hamilton.

What circumstances are crowding you to Christ right now? Can you "rejoice greatly" that these things force you to lean on your Lord? Recognize that the testing of your faith is more precious than refined gold.

Thank you, God, for crowding me into the arms of your Son, Jesus Christ. May I learn to see my troubles as merely "mud around the gold."

DAY 82

Caribbean Pines

Consider it pure joy, my brothers and sisters, whenever you face trials of many kinds, because you know that the testing of your faith produces perseverance. Let perseverance finish its work so that you may be mature and complete, not lacking anything.

—James 1:2–4

The Tamiami Trail is a long, straight highway across Florida's south Everglades. When I drove it with a friend, I was struck by the wild, rugged, oddly beautiful pine trees dotting the landscape. My friend called them Caribbean pines; they are stunning against a South Florida sunset. Unlike tall, straight pines, they are wiry, contorted, and primitive looking. Caribbean pines routinely withstand long periods of drought and fire, and they hold their own against the fiercest of hurricanes. In fact, these particular trees seem to love a rugged environment. They cannot tolerate cultivation. When they are protected, planted in a yard, and given water and fertilizer, they often die. Experts can't pinpoint why Caribbean pines do best in the wild, but they know enough to warn landscapers against using them in a decorative, cultivated setting.

We are like Caribbean pines. Our souls usually don't thrive during good times. Our hearts grow complacent, our need of God becomes less urgent, our hope of heaven dims, and our prayer life often dries up. We may be planted in a beautiful setting with our needs met and every resource at our fingertips, but our soul shrivels. It seems we need an occasional blast of storm or fiery trial, if our faith is to mature.

Are you in a hurricane? Experiencing a drought? A fiery trial? You certainly don't need to ask God to bring on the hardships, but you can ask Jesus for a closer walk with him in the midst of the difficulties you are experiencing (I would guess there are plenty of them). As you hold on to Jesus today, your soul will thrive both in good times and bad.

Lord Jesus, thank you for creating so many examples in nature that inspire us to trust you. Help me to see lessons in your beautiful world around me.

Our souls usually don't thrive during good times. Our hearts grow complacent, our need of God becomes less urgent, our hope of heaven dims, and our prayer life often dries up.

DAY 83

God's Idea of Good

For the L*ORD* *God is a sun and shield; the* L*ORD* *gives grace and glory; no good thing does He withhold from those who walk uprightly. O* L*ORD* *of hosts, how blessed is the man who trusts in You!*

—PSALM 84:11–12 NASB

I learned those verses from Psalm 84 when I was a teenager. I relished the thought, *No good thing does he withhold*. . . . The way I figured it, I just needed to do my homework, finish my chores, keep myself from spats with my sisters, be nice to Aunt Kitty, go to church, say my prayers . . . and . . . and. . . I assumed that if I kept my nose clean, God would give me good grades, good friends, a good college to attend, and good knees to last me through field hockey season. We think that if we are obedient, God will give us financial blessings or trials that can be easily managed. If we do our part, God will dole out the good. Won't he?

I've lived long enough in this wheelchair to know that sometimes our idea of "good" is very different from God's. So how do we read Psalm 84? If our walk is blameless, God will not withhold peace. He will not withhold virtue or faith or courage. He will not withhold grace when we come to him in need. We will be able to run spiritually and not grow weary; we'll be able to walk in faith and not faint. He will not withhold opportunities to sow his seed, to shine his light. He will not withhold patience or endurance or the favor of his nearness and sweetness. He will not withhold the gift of heaven-sent joy. None of these things will he withhold from those who walk uprightly.

Some of God's best gifts must be unwrapped in the darkness. Think of your last major trial. What "good thing" did the Lord slip into your hands in those difficult days?

Lord, lift my gaze to see life from your perspective. Help me to understand—and treasure—every good thing you send from heaven.

DAY 84

In Everything . . . for Everything

Speaking to one another with psalms, hymns, and songs from the Spirit. Sing and make music from your heart to the Lord, always giving thanks to God the Father for everything, in the name of our Lord Jesus Christ.

—EPHESIANS 5:19–20

Once I was discussing the subject of gratitude with a friend who had broken her ankle. For her, being on crutches wasn't fun. There were many appointments and travel plans she had to cancel. "I can accept a verse like 1 Thessalonians 5:18, 'Give thanks *in* all circumstances. . .'" she sighed, looking at her leg cast, "but I don't think I could give thanks *for* this clunky thing."

Something about her comment troubled me. People are willing to thank God *in* the midst of their circumstances for his grace, comfort, and sustaining power. But they draw a line when it comes to the circumstances themselves. We segregate God from the suffering he allows, as though a broken ankle merely "happens," and God shows up after the fact. We don't thank God for the problem, just for finding him in it.

But these verses in Ephesians underscore the supreme sovereignty of God over all suffering. The apostle Paul—who endured his share of tragedies—never considered his circumstances as tragic. He tells all believers we should be "always giving thanks to God the Father *for* everything, in the name of our Lord Jesus Christ" (italics mine).

I give God thanks for my quadriplegia. It has become the strange friend that helps me know Jesus better. It is the shadowy companion that walks with me daily, pulling and pushing me into the arms of the Savior where I find grace and comfort. Your affliction falls well within the overarching decrees of God. It comes from his wise and kind hand, and for that, you can give thanks. In it and for it.

Sovereign God, today I bring my affliction and disappointment before your throne. I thank you in it … for it … and ultimately I thank you for bringing me through it. Please increase a spirit of gratitude that I might always be thankful.

DAY 85

Remember

He allowed no one to oppress them . . . The Lord made his people very fruitful. . . . He brought out Israel, laden with silver and gold. . . . He spread out a cloud as a covering, and a fire to give light at night. . . . He . . . fed them well with the bread of heaven. He opened the rock and water gushed out. . . . He remembered his holy promise given to his servant Abraham. . . . Praise the Lord.

—Psalm 105:14, 24, 37, 39, 40–42, 45

Emotions are one of the least reliable yet influential forces in our lives. One day, we are hopeful; the next, we hate. Despair at one time; delight, the other. Emotions are the surging, restless tides that keep ebbing and flowing, drawing us up, then pushing us down.

The Psalms are a gyroscope, keeping moving things level, like a ship held steady in turbulent seas. This is why the Psalms often repeat the admonition to "*remember* the wonders he has done, his miracles, and the judgments he pronounced" (Psalm 105:5).

My friend used to say, "Never doubt in the darkness what you once believed in the light." When hardship settles in, dark and brooding emotions can surge over us in a tide of doubt and fear. The only sure dike against a flood of glum feelings is to remember. We must recall sunnier times when we drove the pilings of God's goodness deep in our hearts. Happier times when we felt our moorings of trust hold ground. When we lived on his blessings, knew his favor, were grateful for his gifts, and felt the flesh and blood of his everlasting arms underneath us. This is what all forty-five verses of Psalm 105 call us to do.

While it is light, write down things you know to be true. When darkness comes, pull out your list and remember what your feelings have forgotten!

Lord, you are the Light of the World. Help me to remember your kindness and goodness to me when the horizon on my life begins to darken. Thank you for Psalm 105.

DAY 86

Sweeter Than the Day Before

Salvation is nearer now than when we first believed.

—Romans 13:11

It's true. My salvation is so much dearer, sweeter, and nearer to me than when I first believed as a teenager. I appreciated what Jesus had done when I was new in the faith, but I never considered him . . . precious. Only old hymn writers spoke of him as precious! Now *I* am old. And Jesus is my true Friend, my Fortress when I am frightened, my Beloved when I give him praise, my Righteousness when I have sinned, the Shepherd who seeks me when I've gone astray.

How did Jesus become so precious to me? I look at it this way: *Today is the first day of the rest of my salvation*! The Christian idea of salvation involves the past, present, and future. Ephesians 2:8 says, "By grace you *have been saved*, through faith" (italics mine). First Corinthians 1:18 explains that the gospel is the power of God "to us who *are being saved*" (italics mine). Romans 13:11 says, "*Salvation is nearer now* than when we first believed" (italics mine). We have been saved. We are being saved. And we will be saved. At every stage we are saved by the death of Christ. In the past, our sins were paid for by Christ on the cross. In the present, the death of Jesus secures the power of God's Spirit to save us from the domination of sin. And in the future, it will be the blood of Christ that saves us from the wrath of God and ushers us into perfection and joy eternal.

As the old gospel song goes, "Every day with Jesus is sweeter than the day before!"[11] Grasp the sweetness of all that the death of Christ purchased for you in the past, present, and future. Today, get actively engaged in your present salvation, and praise the Lord that you will be saved from the wrath to come.

Precious Jesus, I humbly bow before you, thanking you for all that your death on the cross purchased for me. I want to honor you by obeying you today.

DAY 87

In Weakness, Made Strong

He was crucified in weakness, yet he lives by God's power. Likewise, we are weak in him, yet by God's power we will live with him in our dealing with you.

—2 CORINTHIANS 13:4

Back in 1967 missionary Doug Nichols fell ill while serving in India and had to spend several months in a dingy tuberculosis sanitarium. While there, he tried to give gospel tracts to the patients and doctors, but no one would accept them. Understandably, Doug became discouraged. He was sick, weak, lonely, and disappointed no one would listen to him.

One night around 2:00 a.m., Doug woke up coughing. Across the aisle, he noticed an old man trying to get out of bed and get to the bathroom. Too weak to stand, the man fell back into bed crying and exhausted. Although sick himself and as weak as he had ever been, Doug got out of bed and with a smile placed one arm under the patient's neck and the other under his legs. With all his strength he lifted the man and carried him down the hall to the filthy, smelly washroom. Then the missionary carried him back to his bed. The old man smiled and said the Indian word for "thanks."

What happened the next morning was amazing. One of the other patients woke Doug up with a steaming cup of tea, making motions that he wanted a gospel tract. Then other patients asked for the booklets. Even nurses and a doctor asked for one. Over the next few days, several patients and staff gave their lives to Christ. The whole situation changed because of Doug's sacrificial act in the middle of the night.

The power of the good news is released in your life when you allow your weaknesses to showcase the awesome might and love of our Savior. Plan on doing that today.

Father, I confess that I pass by opportunities to help others in the name of Jesus because I just don't want to get involved or don't want to get my hands dirty. Move me, by your Spirit, to reach beyond my own strength.

DAY 88

Thanks, but No Thanks

Give thanks to the L*ORD*, *for he is good.*
His love endures forever.
—PSALM 136:1

I learned early on in my disability how important it is to say, "Thank you." So many people do so many things *for* me or *to* me. Someone has to help me into bed, help me out of bed, pour the coffee, get me dressed, brush my hair, brush my teeth, blow my nose . . . and I am quick to say, "Thank you for helping me." And I mean it. What's more, I say it a lot. The other day my friend Judy came into my office and asked if she could borrow ten dollars. I was busy and absentmindedly told her to take it out of my wallet, which she did. When I heard my purse snap shut, I automatically said in a cheery voice, "Thank you!" Judy gave me the strangest look and another friend standing nearby said, "What did you thank her for? She's the one who ought to thank you!" It was an odd thing for me to say, but I guess I'm just programmed to express my gratitude to people.

Oh, were it only that way with the Lord Jesus! If only we were better "programmed" to be more grateful to God, to lift prayers countless of times during a day, saying, "Thank you, Lord, for this . . ." and "I am so grateful to you, Jesus, for that . . ."

The entire Psalm 136 is a litany of thanks to God and a wonderful portion of Scripture to remember when you are suffering. When life hurts, it's often hard to be grateful for anything, yet what a display of God's power when others see you give thanks in tough situations.

I give thanks to you, dear Father, for choosing me to be a part of your eternal family. I give thanks to you, precious Jesus, for rescuing me out of the kingdom of darkness through your death and resurrection. And I give thanks to you, Holy Spirit, for applying to me, and all the church, every benefit of salvation.

DAY 89

She Did What She Could

"Leave her alone," said Jesus. "Why are you bothering her? She has done a beautiful thing to me.... She did what she could. She poured perfume on my body beforehand to prepare for my burial. Truly I tell you, wherever the gospel is preached throughout the world, what she has done will also be told, in memory of her."

—MARK 14:6, 8–9

When it comes to the Christian life, the stakes are high. Things like heaven, hell, and eternal reward. You and I get only one chance on earth to live a life pleasing to our Master. No starting over and no reincarnation. We have been given life and breath to prove our faith and demonstrate what we believe. It's why I sometimes wake up at night, wondering, *Am I doing this thing called "the Christian life" right? Am I making the most of the moments God gives me?*

I found a calming, reassuring answer the other day in Mark 14. When the woman poured expensive perfume on Jesus' head, some people at the banquet thought she did a stupid thing. But Jesus rebuked them harshly and said, "Leave her alone . . . she did what she could do . . . and I think it's beautiful." I identified with the woman. I feel like I have often done stupid things in my service to the Lord. *Am I doing this right? Is this pleasing to God?* But like the woman in Mark 14, I did what I could. And that's all God asks. We can only do what we are able to do; but inspired by the Spirit, it's always a beautiful thing in Jesus' sight.

"She did what she could—Mark 14" is written on the tombstone of Fanny Crosby, the blind composer of over four thousand hymns. Don't have anxious thoughts about the high stakes involved in Christian service. Just ask for the Spirit's help and do what you are able to do. Jesus will think it's beautiful.

> Holy Spirit, empower me this day so I can do what I'm able to do in service to my Master.

DAY 90

Divine Distastes

And he could bear Israel's misery no longer.

—JUDGES 10:16

God has a strong distaste for suffering. His tenderness is aroused by human anguish. *But what about all of those natural disasters? you wonder. If God's so touched by suffering, why does he allow terrible tsunamis that sweep away whole villages? Why devastating earthquakes that flatten a city? In catastrophes like these, the suffering and loss of life is beyond comprehension.*

I can't begin to explain the unexplainable. But I know this: If Adam had never fallen, if the Creator could rewrite the story, he would have never allowed suffering out of the cage. "For he does not willingly bring affliction or grief to anyone" (Lamentations 3:33). But sin did leave the cage, and consequently the curse fell. And ever since man's rebellion in the garden of Eden, our world has groaned under wars, floods, earthquakes, diseases, and much more. Like you, I shake my head at the mysterious plans and purposes of God. Tragedies like these either drive people away from God . . . or draw them to him. Calamities either harden people's hearts . . . or soften them as they run to the Lord for help and hope.

And beyond all else, I know this about my Father's heart: "God put his love on the line for us by offering his Son in sacrificial death while we were of no use whatever to him." And again, "God didn't hesitate to put everything on the line for us, embracing our condition and exposing himself to the worst by sending his own Son" (Romans 5:8; 8:32 THE MESSAGE).

No one could ever accuse God of "sitting back and watching" while people suffer. How could anyone look at the cross and say anything like that?

Tragedies, great and small, happen every day in your community! How can you become God's hands and feet, his tender touch and his encouraging voice to those who suffer in your city—and in your world? Ask him to express his compassion toward hurting people through you.

Father, may I simply trust your heart, even today, when I can't trace your path.

DAY 91

Yours for a Song

Jehoshaphat appointed men to sing to the LORD and to praise him for the splendor of his holiness as they went out at the head of the army, saying: "Give thanks to the LORD, for his love endures forever." As they began to sing and praise, the LORD set ambushes against the men of Ammon and Moab and Mount Seir who were invading Judah, and they were defeated.

—2 CHRONICLES 20:21–22

People facing fear have often resorted to song. But for God's people, it's not any old song. When King Jehoshaphat was confronted by a great force of allied armies, he had his people fast, pray, and then he assembled the troops . . . placing the choir out in front of the army! As they marched, the singers lifted up praise to the beauty of God's holiness. And as they sang and praised the Lord, the opposition was thrown into confusion.

Songs and hymns of praise clear the air like nothing else. If you're in any kind of spiritual conflict, the best *defense* is to sing. It's a way of resisting the devil. Singing is also the best *offense*. Songs of praise will confuse the Enemy and send the devil's hoards hightailing. Amy Carmichael, missionary to India, wrote: "I truly believe Satan cannot endure the power of song and so slips out of the room . . . when there is a hymn of praise. Prayer rises more easily, more spontaneously, after one has let those wings, words and music, carry one out of oneself into that upper air."[12]

Victory over the Enemy can be yours for a song! Sing a hymn or a worship chorus as you march into your day or wrap up your evening. And if you can't sing, read one of David's praise psalms out loud. To begin and end the day with God's praise will do much to chase away dark thoughts, and open the door to peace.

Lord, you are worthy of endless praise. Help me to make room in my thoughts for the songs that declare your greatness and love before both men and angels.

Songs and hymns of praise clear the air like nothing else. If you're in any kind of spiritual conflict, the best defense is to sing.

DAY 92

Finishing Well

For I am already being poured out like a drink offering, and the time for my departure is near. I have fought the good fight, I have finished the race, I have kept the faith. . . . Do your best to come to me quickly, for Demas, because he loved this world, has deserted me and has gone to Thessalonica. Crescens has gone to Galatia, and Titus to Dalmatia. Only Luke is with me.

—2 TIMOTHY 4:6–7, 9–11

The book of Acts records the golden days of Paul's ministry. It seemed no effort for him to be wide awake at midnight in a jail cell, praying despite his biting chains and singing hymns at the top of his lungs. Scripture tells us the jail doors flew open wide, and everyone's chains fell off. Prisoners applauded him and the jail keeper, saved instantly, invited him to his house. Things were looking up!

But if you look closer at his last epistle, you see a softer side. Paul was in jail again when he wrote 2 Timothy. But this time there was no miracle, no escape. Winter was approaching and Paul felt old and tired. Deserted by his friends, he struggled against sickness. His friend Trophimus was sick, yet Paul couldn't do a thing to heal his friend. He couldn't even heal himself!

Yet the old apostle didn't allow discouraging circumstances to get him down. Things were different than the "golden days of old," yet he hung on courageously to God.

Some days you feel life is on the upswing, other days it's flat. Sometimes you sense the miracle in your life, other times life seems very ordinary. Are you energized today to meet a challenge head-on? Or do you feel tired and trapped? Life's circumstances can make you feel like a yo-yo, but don't allow the "ups and downs" to get you down. Commit to God to fight the good fight . . . finish the race . . . keep the faith.

Give me strength, Lord, to finish well and not allow life's disappointments, along with age, aches, and pains to dampen my trust.

DAY 93

The Real Tragedy

In him we were also chosen, having been predestined according to the plan of him who works out everything in conformity with the purpose of his will.

—EPHESIANS 1:11

It's one thing for God to deliberately let something awful happen for reasons we may not understand, but it would be another for God to wish he could have prevented it but have one hand tied behind his back. Either God rules, or Satan sets your life's agenda, and God is limited to only reacting. In which case, the Almighty would become the devil's cleanup boy. Although God would manage to patch things up, your suffering would be meaningless. One Christian writer who believes that God has little to do with the specific circumstances that come your way expressed it like this: "In 1982 someone laced capsules of the pain reliever Tylenol with cyanide and then put them back on store shelves in Chicago. Seven people died after swallowing poisoned pills, the families of those seven people no doubt agonized trying to find some shred of meaning in why God or fate or luck had picked on their loved ones, of all the people in Chicago. We can concoct some answer and perhaps take some small comfort in it, but sadly, *there was no meaning in those deaths. Each was a bizarre, horrible coincidence, nothing more*. Therein lies the tragedy."[13]

No, the real tragedy is that any Christian would settle for such darkness with the light of the Bible shining so clearly. If God didn't control evil, the result would be evil uncontrolled. Our suffering has meaning because "his kingdom rules over all" (Psalm 103:19).

We may not grasp it this side of eternity, but if his kingdom rules over all—and it does—that includes the tiniest details of your life. Praise God that evil has a governor—our great and wise God.

Lord God, I am grateful that you purpose and permit. You give suffering meaning simply because you and you alone are in control!

DAY 94

In Jesus' Name

I will do whatever you ask in my name.... You may ask me for anything in my name, and I will do it.

—JOHN 14:13–14

These are profound words from the lips of Jesus. Let's examine his promise closely. "I will do whatever you ask *in my name*." What does that mean? Surely, more than saying "In Jesus' name" at the end of a prayer just before saying the amen. To pray in the name of Jesus is to pray admitting that God hears me only because I'm the guest of his Son. It's to pray in the bold but respectful way that Jesus did while on earth.

To pray in Jesus' name is to ask God for the things Jesus taught us to. He summarizes them in the Lord's Prayer: spiritual things, eternal things. "May your kingdom spread. . . . May your plans be accomplished on this rebellious planet. . . . Forgive the way I've treated you. . . . Keep me from falling for the evil that allures me" (Matthew 6:9–13). Only one request in six deals with earthbound matters, and even there he taught us to pray, "Give us this day our daily bread" —not, "Bless the Dow Jones average and please be with the NASDAQ in the next financial quarter."

Of course it's not wrong to pray beyond our basic needs—to pray that Susie will find her lost kitten, that none of us will catch colds this winter, and that Christmas will hurry up and get here. God loves to hear preschoolers pray. But Jesus also invites grown-ups to "cast all your anxiety on him," and "pray about everything" (1 Peter 5:7; Philippians 4:6 NLV). But do we really think Jesus gave us a blank check for an easy life? Do we imagine we can pray our way clear of trials? Think again, and "in your thinking be adults" (1 Corinthians 14:20).

Your name is precious, Jesus, and I want to come before you in prayer and ask for the sorts of things that are on your heart. Give me your ideas in prayer.

DAY 95

Lifesaving Truth

As for you, you were dead in your transgressions and sins.

—Ephesians 2:1

I once heard Dr. R. C. Sproul paint a fascinating picture of how "dead in sin" we are. He described the unbeliever as lying "flat-dead-drowned" on the bottom of a pool under six feet of water. The man is so dead he can't possibly hear the "good news" that a lifesaver is on the way. He can't respond. God is the Lifesaver who must reach down, pull the unbeliever out of the water, and breathe life into his dead body. Once quickened, the man happily recognizes his Savior, reaches up, and embraces him. That's the gospel.

There are two different interpretations of the gospel. One makes salvation dependent on the work of God, the other on a work of man. One regards faith as part of God's gift of salvation, the other sees faith as man's own contribution to salvation. One gives all the glory of saving to God; the other divides the praise between God who "built the machinery" of salvation, and man who operated it by believing.

John 1:13 underscores that we are spiritually born "not of natural descent, nor of human decision or a husband's will, but born of God." We are made alive out of the deadness of our sin by the will of God, for Jesus said, "You did not choose me, but I chose you" (John 15:16).

As much as it goes against our natural grain, we are not masters of our own fate or captains of our own souls. Throughout this day, rehearse in your heart that (1) all men are sinners and cannot do anything to save themselves; (2) Jesus Christ, God's Son, is a perfect Savior for sinners, even the worst; and (3) the Father and the Son have promised that all who know themselves to be sinners and place their faith in Christ the Savior shall be received into favor and no one cast away.

Father, I praise you for quickening my spirit and giving me saving faith that I might recognize Jesus as my Savior!

DAY 96

You're a Jewel!

The LORD their God will save his people on that day as a shepherd saves his flock. They will sparkle in his land like jewels in a crown.
—ZECHARIAH 9:16

The Bible gives us this unusual detail about the construction of the Lord's temple: "In building the temple, only blocks dressed at the quarry were used, and no hammer, chisel or any other iron tool was heard at the temple site while it was being built" (1 Kings 6:7). An unbelievable amount of scraping, hammering, and chiseling had to be done on those mighty rocks that were used in the construction. But it was all done out of view and out of earshot of the temple site.

It's a little like the way God "dresses" us, fitting us for heaven. The apostle Peter reminds us that you and I are living stones, and we are being mined in the quarry of earth, a place of noise, chiseling, and clouds of dust. God is using our sufferings and afflictions to hone and shape us so we might fit perfectly into heaven's landscape, where there is "no hammer, chisel or any other iron tool." Where there is no suffering. No tears, pain, sorrow, or death. As polished stones, not only will we fit in heaven, we will fit as glittering jewels in his crown. Soon we will enter the utter serenity of heaven—a place of peace and quiet—and God will set us in his diadem as sparkling and dazzling jewels.

God's quarry is still busy. He is active with his hammer and chisel in your life, honing you and shaping you for a high and eternal destiny. The shaping isn't always easy. How well I know! But take heart today, friend. Bear a bit longer with the noise and hammering. Serve others while you wait. One day all of heaven will be in awe over what the Master Jeweler has accomplished in your life.

Lord, even though I am still in process, still being shaped and chiseled, I pray that your radiant beauty would shine through my life today.

DAY 97

Salvation Is of the Lord

Here I am! I stand at the door and knock. If anyone hears my voice and opens the door, I will come in and eat with that person, and they with me.

—Revelation 3:20

I love the painting of Jesus standing at a door with a lamp in one hand and gently knocking with the other. When you look closely, you see there is no doorknob. The suggestion is that the door can only be opened from the inside, placing the responsibility of salvation on the person behind the door. It's a lovely painting inspired by Revelation 3:20 (which is actually an invitation of fellowship to believers, not an invitation of salvation to unbelievers).

The true picture of salvation is that we are utterly dead in our sin. We are spiritually deaf and cannot even hear Jesus knocking. A more accurate picture might be Jesus rapping on the door, climbing over it, and then placing our lifeless hand on the inside doorknob! Jesus is the One who gives us the faith to believe (Romans 12:3). He unplugs our ears, opens our eyes, touches our hearts, illumines our thinking, and plants within us saving faith to say, "I believe!"

Ephesians 2:8–9 says, "For it is by grace you have been saved, through faith—and this not from yourselves, it is the gift of God—not by works, so that no one can boast." The spiritual mind would rather speak of conversion in a way that makes plain whose work it really was: "Salvation belongs to our God," says Revelation 7:10.

Jesus says in John 6:44 that "no one can come to me unless the Father who sent me draws them." When we insist "I made up my mind to be a Christian," it indicates a will that believes it has played a major role in salvation. The truth is, "apart from [Jesus] you can do nothing" (John 15:5)—not even secure your own eternal life.

Lord, thank you that you awakened me out of complete spiritual lifelessness to give me the gift of salvation.

DAY 98

Apples of Gold

Like apples of gold in settings of silver is a ruling rightly given.

—PROVERBS 25:11

My friend Gail MacDonald makes a habit of collecting short sayings of encouragement from saints of old. Whether it's a quote from a missionary or a line from a time-honored hymn, Gail realizes that a few wise words go a long way in lifting one's vision and stretching one's faith. When an envelope arrives in the mail with her familiar handwriting, I know I'm about to be blessed.

Once when I came home from a long, rigorous trip overseas, I spotted a letter from Gail on my kitchen table. I quickly opened it, read her words of greeting, and then enjoyed several lines from Amy Carmichael, the notable missionary: "There is no need to plead that the love of God shall fill our heart as though he were unwilling to fill us. He is willing as light is willing to flood a room that is opened to its brightness; willing as water is willing to flow into an emptied channel. Love is pressing round us on all sides like air. Cease to resist and instantly love takes possession."[14]

Those were golden words to me, especially after a long trip. I was tired, weary, and in need of a fresh perspective. Proverbs 20:15 describes Gail perfectly, "Gold there is, and rubies in abundance, but lips that speak knowledge are a rare jewel."

Like my friend Gail, I am a collector of precious yet sturdy quotes penned by saints of old, including Spurgeon, many Puritan writers, and contemporaries like John Piper. I keep a file of clippings for those seasons in life when I feel overwhelmed or discouraged by pain. Start collecting timely quotes that have bolstered your spirits. Build a file folder of these, and you'll have plenty of words of encouragement to savor in the months to come.

Lord Jesus, you are the Word and only you have the words of life. May I treasure every lifegiving encouragement that comes from you and others today, whether in notes, texts, or emails. And give me the strength to pass blessed words on to those who hurt.

DAY 99

Come Quickly

The Spirit and the bride say, "Come!" And let the one who hears say, "Come!" Let the one who is thirsty come; and let the one who wishes take the free gift of the water of life.

—REVELATION 22:17

The writers of the New Testament were a bruised and battered bunch. This is why they wrote so much about heaven. The hope of heaven stoked fire in their bones, and their writings were laced with constant references to the second coming of Christ, to the time when their Savior would restore all things and complete the kingdom. Continually they were praying, "Maranatha! Come, Lord Jesus!" They were eagerly waiting for Jesus Christ to be revealed (1 Corinthians 1:7).

These suffering saints weren't trying to escape the painful realities of earth; they gladly endured their hardships. They were able to be happy because they knew heaven would reveal the earthshaking significance behind each tear and affliction. They likened themselves to soldiers poised on the watchtower, workers hoeing for the harvest, athletes straining toward the finish line, and virgins waiting wide-eyed in the night, lamps trimmed, hearts afire, and scanning the horizon for the arrival of their beloved. For New Testament writers who suffered—and suffered much—the world was no party. Rather, they were anticipating the coming Party.

We say "Come, Lord Jesus" with one breath, but in the next, we must always pray, "And until you return, give me grace to bear up under my hardship, peace to accept my life circumstances, and courage to tell others about Jesus Christ so that they too can joyously anticipate the Savior's return." So "strengthen the feeble hands, steady the knees that give way; say to those with fearful hearts, 'Be strong, do not fear; your God will come . . . he will come to save you'" (Isaiah 35:3–4).

Lord Jesus, I recognize that this earth can never keep its promises; it can never satisfy. Help me to set my heart on heavenly glories above. Help me to make sure I invite others to that heavenly Party!

DAY 100

Amen

Here is a trustworthy saying: If we died with him, we will also live with him; if we endure, we will also reign with him. If we disown him, he will also disown us; if we are faithless, he will remain faithful, for he cannot disown himself.

—2 TIMOTHY 2:11–13

What a great verse on which to end this book. For here is a trustworthy saying: It really is all about Jesus. We've covered so many promises of God in these pages, and every one of them—every single verse—points in some way to Jesus. He *is* the Word of Life (1 John 1:1). Revelation 22:13 frames Jesus with these timeless words, for the Savior himself proclaims, "I am the Alpha and the Omega, the First and the Last, the Beginning and the End."

What more can we say? Who else would we turn to? There is no one like Jesus. And I think I can hear you say "Amen!" to that.

Second Corinthians 1:20 (KJV) says, "For all the promises of God in him are yea, and in him Amen, unto the glory of God by us." Amen signifies "so be it!" Every promise of God that has blessed you ultimately finds its conclusion in Christ. Every insight and bit of wisdom you've garnered, every obedience you've learned, every step higher into a more prayerful life, *all of it* finds its center—it's beginning and end—in Jesus Christ.

It is my prayer that you keep keeping faith when life is hard. I pray that the plans, decisions, and choices you make, the way you spend your time, the thoughts you entertain and the company you keep, the manner in which you live before others, *all of it* will point to Jesus. May his glory go before you through every trial and test of your faith!

Jesus Christ ... Son of God ... Lord of heaven and earth ... in the days ahead, help me to showcase your glory and greatness in fresh new ways. And to this, I say, "Amen! So be it!"

Notes

1. "A Willing Captive," *Tabletalk* (Ligonier Ministries, October 1997), 20.
2. Dan Allender and Tremper Longman III, *The Cry of the Soul: How Our Emotions Reveal Our Deepest Questions About God (*NavPress, 1994), 72.
3. Paul David Tripp, *You Are Never Alone in the Dark* (Christian Counseling and Educational Foundation, n.d.), 5.
4. Dan Allender and Tremper Longman III, *The Cry of the Soul: How Our Emotions Reveal Our Deepest Questions About God* (NavPress, 1994), 74.
5. John Piper, "Brokenhearted Joy," *World Magazine*, December 13, 2003, 51.
6. Jonathan Edwards, *Heaven: A World of Love* (Calvary Press, 1992), 26.
7. John Bunyan, *The Acceptable Sacrifice: The Excellency of a Broken Heart, in The Works of John Bunyan*, vol. 1, (Banner of Truth Trust, 1992), 720.
8. Søren Kierkegaard, *Upbuilding Discourses in Various Spirits* (Princeton University Press, 1992), 104.
9. Frank Darabont, dir., *The Shawshank Redemption* (Warner Bros., 1994), film.
10. E. Margaret Clarkson, "*In Pain,*" *Grace Grows Best in Winter* (Grand Rapids, Mich.: Eerdmans), 54.
11. Wendell P. Loveless, "Every Day with Jesus" (1936).

12. Amy Carmichael, "Not in Vain," *Mountain Breezes* (Christian Literature Crusade, 1999), 295.
13. John Boykin, *Circumstances and the Role of God (*Zondervan, 1986), 42.
14. Amy Carmichael, quoted in *Draper's Book of Quotations for the Christian World,* ed. Edythe Draper (Tyndale House Publishers, 1992), 259.

How to Contact Joni

After becoming paralyzed at age 17, Joni Eareckson Tada discovered that sometimes "God permits what he hates to accomplish what he loves." She couldn't imagine how God would use her faith to reach suffering people worldwide . . .

In 1979 Joni founded Joni and Friends®, which is now an international disability ministry that sees and meets the needs of people with disabilities, all in the name of Jesus. Since its beginning, Joni and Friends has been sharing the Good News of Jesus and working toward the vision of a world where every person with a disability finds hope, dignity, and their place in the body of Christ.

The Joni and Friends *Wheels for the World®* program delivers wheelchairs and Bibles to people with disabilities in developing nations. Through *Joni's House®* programs, we provide Christ-centered care to meet the critical needs of people with disabilities in their local communities. And across the United States, and in countries around the world, our teams host *Retreats & Getaways* and care year-round for families living with disability, connecting them with local service providers and inclusive Christ-honoring churches.

So, get involved! Pray for and support Joni and Friends as we carry out our biblical commission found in Luke 14:21, 23: "Go out quickly in the streets and alleys of the town and bring in the poor, the crippled, the blind and the lame. . . . Go out to the roads and country lanes and compel them to come in, so that my house will be full." (NIV)

Reach out to us at www.joniandfriends.org.